# Collins
# Artist's Little Book
# of Watercolour

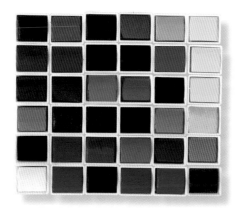

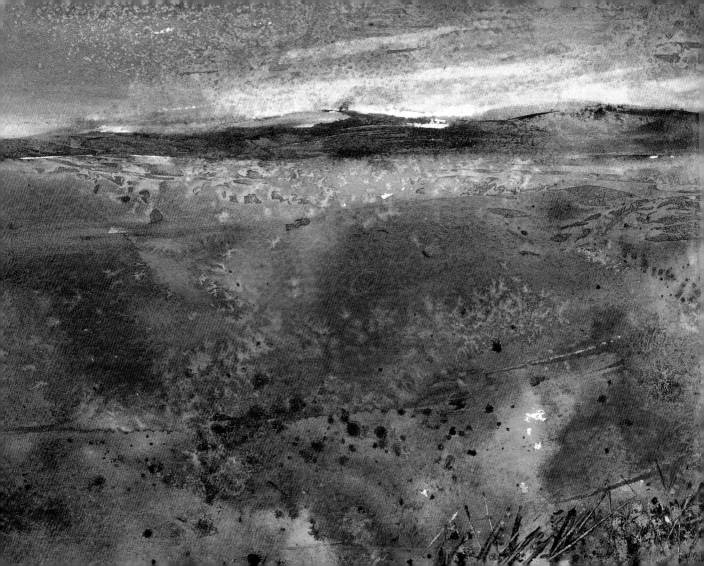

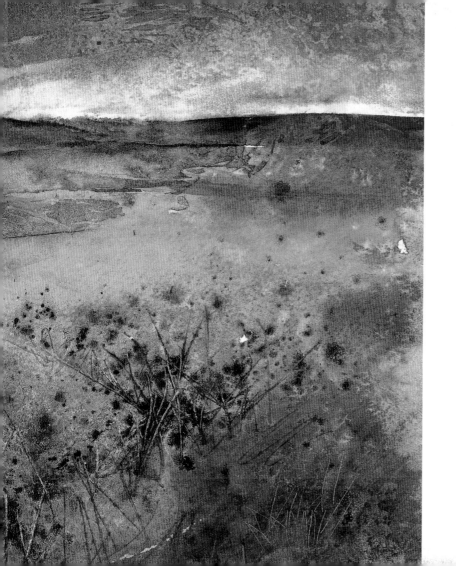

# Collins
# Artist's
# Little Book of
# Watercolour

## Simon Jennings

Collins

First published in 2008
by Collins,
an imprint of
HarperCollins Publishers
77–85 Fulham Palace Road
Hammersmith, London W6 8JB

12  11  10  09  08
5   4   3   2   1

Based on material from *Collins Complete Artist's Manual*

Collins is a registered trademark of HarperCollins Publishers Limited

**Previous page:**
**Ann Blockley**
*Imagine (detail)*
**Watercolour on paper**
**27 x 39 cm (10½ x 15¼ in)**

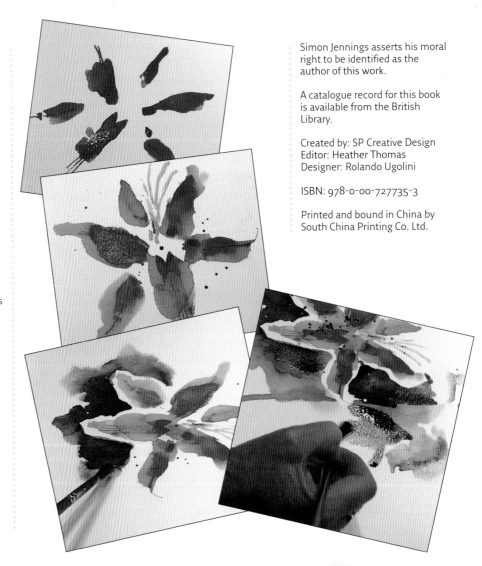

Simon Jennings asserts his moral right to be identified as the author of this work.

A catalogue record for this book is available from the British Library.

Created by: SP Creative Design
Editor: Heather Thomas
Designer: Rolando Ugolini

ISBN: 978-0-00-727735-3

Printed and bound in China by South China Printing Co. Ltd.

Collins
# Artist's Little Book of Watercolour

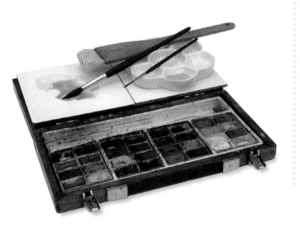

# Contents

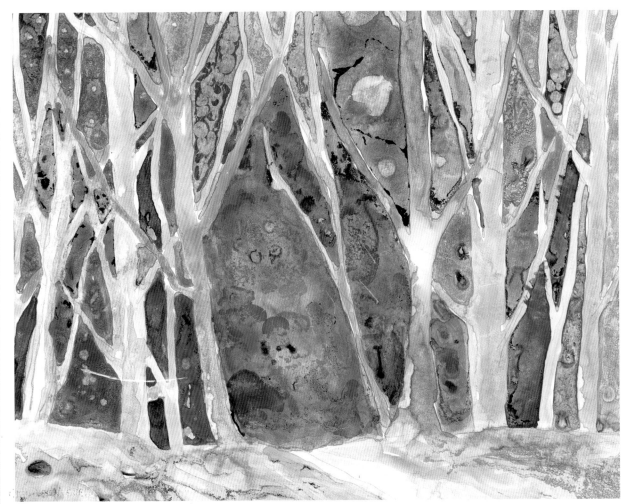

# Introduction

All artists have an urge to communicate their own unique view of the world, and one of the beauties of watercolour as a medium is its immediacy – a small paintbox, a sheet of paper and a brush, and you're away. And you only require water to paint and clean up with, which makes watercolour painting feel accessible.

Watercolour invites a direct and spontaneous response to any subject – whether you are painting a landscape, a portrait, a figure study, a still life or an expressive abstract. In fact, no other medium has the same capacity to capture a subject with such speed and economy of brush stroke.

Far and away the most popular of the painting mediums, watercolour is also probably the most challenging and frustrating for artists, even professionals. Its fluid nature makes it much less predictable than other mediums, but this is more than compensated for by the range of exciting and beautiful effects that it can create, sometimes more by accident than design. When it is used well, it can make a clear statement in pure colour.

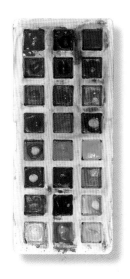

**Fiona Peart**
*Winter Trees*
**Watercolour on paper**
**20 x 26cm (8 x 10in)**

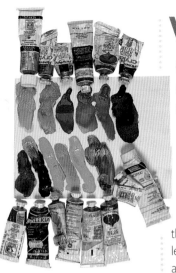

# Why watercolour?

One of the advantages of painting in watercolours is that, being compact and lightweight, they are highly portable. You can paint on top of a mountain, or even on a bus. You need minimal storage space and a single portfolio will house dozens of paintings.

## Making it easy

In spite of its many positive attributes, watercolour, does, however, have some hidden pitfalls, and it is a lot more difficult than it looks. For instance, you have to learn not to fiddle and overwork a painting, as well as developing the knack of building up a painting without making mistakes.

## Invest in the best

Trying to save money when buying your materials is a false economy, and it is worth investing in better-quality paints, paper and brushes. Using the best paints will certainly make working in watercolour easier for you. Although most watercolourists use both tubes and pans, they tend to favour tube colours because they allow you to mix stronger colours more quickly and in larger quantities. However, pans are easier to carry around, and are useful for applying the finishing touches to a picture. It's also more convenient to buy pans of colours you use infrequently.

Good-quality watercolour paper is also essential, otherwise your colours will be flat and lifeless. If you try to economize and use cheap, thin paper, it will cockle.

When you begin to paint regularly, and especially when making larger pictures, you will find that sable brushes, although quite expensive, are worth their weight in gold. Not only do they carry as much colour as you need for one wash but they also will respond sensitively to even the slightest movement of your hand. If your budget is limited, buy one large sable brush rather than several small ones. It will point well for painting details, yet will still have plenty of colour-carrying capacity.

## Other water-based media

Whatever the reasons you might have for choosing a medium, its visual qualities are the most compelling. It's not so much that one medium is more attractive or in some way superior to another, but more to do with the way you feel about a picture when you look at it and how it makes you want to paint your own pictures in a similar medium.

### Gouache

This type of paint used to be known as 'body colour' and was achieved by mixing Chinese white into other watercolours to make them opaque. It was used to give extra solidity and highlights when painting watercolours, or to create paintings from solid colour. Today, the best-quality gouache is highly pigmented, giving dense, matt, opaque colours that flow well and dry without streaks. Watercolourists often use permanent white gouache for highlights.

### Water-soluble pencil

This medium can be useful for beginners in bridging the gap between drawing and painting in watercolours, but the results are not the same as those achieved by applying a conventional colour wash. Like gouache and tempera, a fast-drying water-based medium, they are ideal for sketching on location and making colour notes. Thick water-soluble crayons are capable of making broader marks and denser hatching, making them more of a painter's medium. Brushing water over water-soluble pencil turns a line drawing into a watercolour.

**John Blockley**
*Moorland Road*
**Watercolour on paper**
**30.5 x 46cm**
**(12 x 18in)**

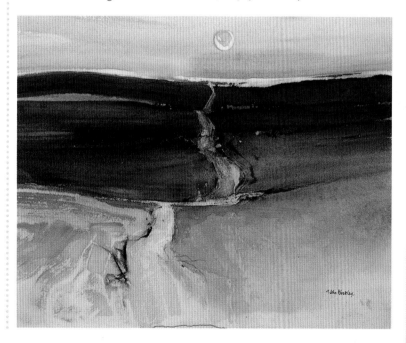

9

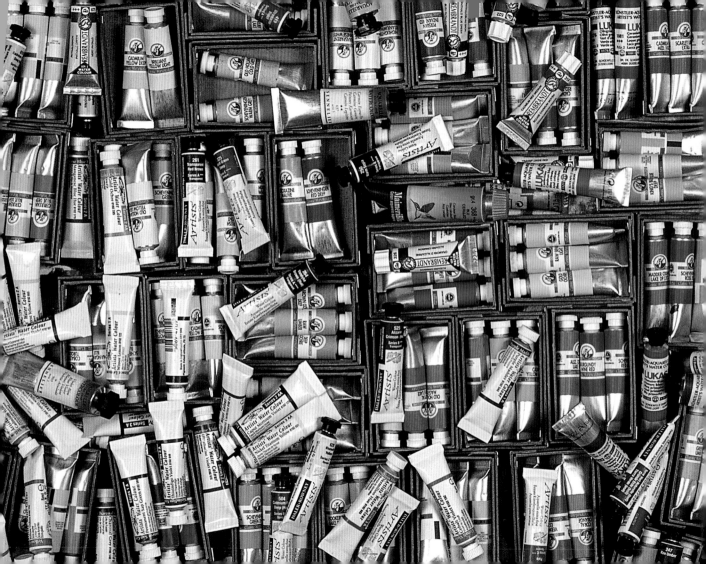

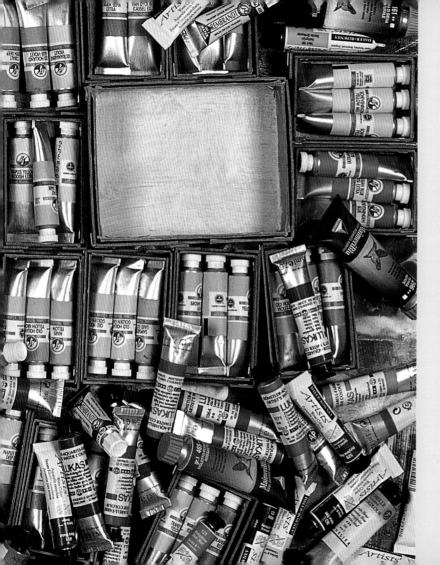

# Paints and pigments

Paints for watercolour consist of very finely ground pigments that are bound with gum-arabic solution. The gum enables the paint to be heavily diluted with water to make thin, transparent washes of colour, without losing adhesion to the support. Glycerine is added to the mixture to improve its solubility and prevent the paint cracking, along with a wetting agent, such as ox gall, to ensure an even flow of paint across the paper.

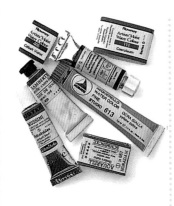

# Choosing and buying paints

It is natural to assume that there is little difference in formulation between one brand of watercolour paint and another. In reality, the types and proportions of ingredients used by manufacturers differ, so there are often variations in consistency, colour strength, handling qualities, and even permanence between paint ranges.

It is worth trying out several brands of paint initially, as you may find that one suits your style of working better than another. You don't have to stick to one brand, however; good-quality watercolour paints are compatible across the ranges, and you may discover that certain individual colours perform better in one range than another. Viridian is a good example: in some brands it has a tendency to be gritty, while in other ranges it is perfectly smooth and clear.

## Types of paint

Watercolours are available in two main forms – as small, compressed blocks of colour, which are called 'pans' or 'half pans' according to their size, and as moist colour in tubes. The formulations of tube and pan colours are very similar, and which

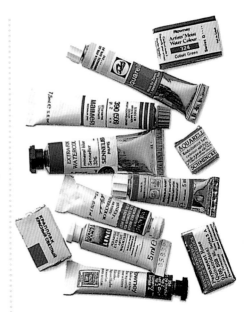

**A selection of watercolours, including pans, half pans and tubes.**

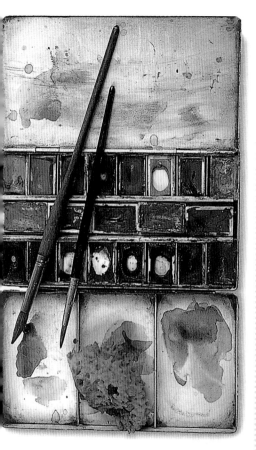

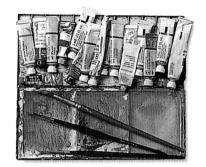

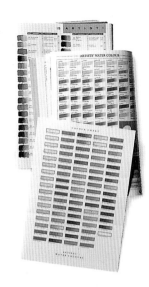

type you choose is a matter of personal preference. Traditional watercolour boxes containing pans are designed to be portable and are ideal for working outdoors on location. Good-quality equipment will repay you with many years of loyal service, so it is never worth trying to cut corners and make false economies when you are purchasing your painting materials.

## Differences between brands

Be aware that colours that are mixtures of pigments, such as sap green and Payne's grey, may show a marked variation in hue between brands because they are formulated differently, so you should not expect a familiar colour name to be exactly the same in a different brand.

**A watercolour box with small pans is light and portable, making it convenient for painting outdoors on location.**

## Using charts

**When buying paints, don't depend on manufacturers' colour charts as a guide to a colour's appearance. Most of them are printed with inks that are not accurate representations of the colours. Handmade tint charts produced with actual paint on swatches of watercolour paper are more reliable; ask your art supplier if they have one you can refer to.**

13

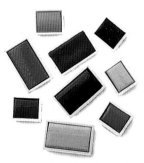

**Pans and half pans**

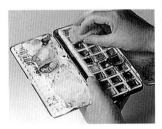

**Preventing lids sticking**
**After a painting session,**
**always remove any excess**
**moisture from the pan**
**colours with a damp sponge.**

# Pans and half pans

Pans and half pans slot neatly into their tailor-made, enamelled-metal boxes with special recesses to hold them in place and separate them, and a lid that doubles as a palette when opened out.

You can either buy boxes containing a range of preselected colours or, preferably, fill an empty box with your own choice of pans. Colour is released by stroking them with a wet brush; the wetter the brush, the lighter the tone obtained.

Pans are light and easy to use when you are painting out of doors. The colours are always in the same position in the box when you want them, and they do not leak. They are also very economical to use, with minimal wastage of paint. However, it takes a little effort to lift enough colour onto the brush. Paints become dirtied when you dart from one to the other without rinsing out your brush in between.

# Care of pans

New pans tend to stick to the inside of the lid when you close the box; when you next open the lid, they may scatter out of order. It is good practice to remove any excess moisture from pans with a damp sponge after a painting session. Leave the box open in a warm room for a few hours to let the colours dry off before closing the lid, and dry the palette on the inside of the lid before closing it, or the paints will absorb the moisture and become sticky.

When using pan colours for the first time, wet them with a drop of water and leave until the water has been absorbed. This will ensure easier paint release when the pans are stroked with the brush.

**Improvised pans**
**Always replace the caps of tube**
**colours immediately, otherwise**
**the paint will harden in the tube.**
**If this does happen, however,**
**just cut open the tube and**
**then you can use it as an**
**improvised pan. So long as**
**the paint is not so old that**
**the gum-arabic binder has**
**become insoluble, it should**
**be possible to reconstitute**
**the paint with some water.**

# Tubes

Tubes of colour are available in sizes ranging from 5–20ml (0.17–0.66 US fl oz), the standard size being 15ml (0.5 US fl oz). The smaller sizes are designed to fit into travelling watercolour boxes, but the bigger tubes are more economical for large-scale work. Tubes can be bought either singly or in pre-selected sets. Choosing your own tubes means that you can obtain precisely the colours you need.

Tube colours are more cumbersome than pans when painting out of doors, but they are more suitable for large-scale work in the studio. Because tube paint is more

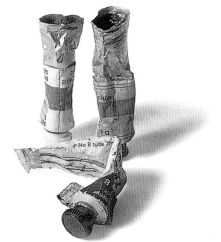

fluid than the equivalent pan form, it is better for mixing large amounts of paint. Tubes can be more wasteful than pan colours, however, because it is easy to squeeze out more paint than you need, and the paint can leak and solidify if the cap is not replaced properly. Tube colour is also prone to settling, as old stock may harden or separate in the tube.

## Care of tubes

Always clean the tube thread before you replace a cap, or it may stick – the gum arabic in the paint acts as a glue. Stuck caps can be opened either with pliers, or by holding the tube under a hot tap so that the cap expands and is easier to remove. Do not throw away tubes of hard paint, as it is often possible to salvage the contents (see below for how to do this).

### Salvaging tubes

**It is possible to bring dried-up tube paint back to its former paste-like consistency. Just unroll the tube and then cut the end off before adding a few drops of water. Now let the hardened paint absorb the moisture, and rework it back to a paste.**

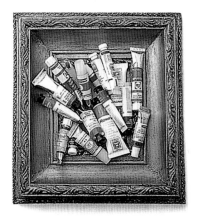

**Standard tube sizes**
**As shown here, tubes of colour are available in several standard sizes. Buy larger tubes of the colours you tend to use frequently.**

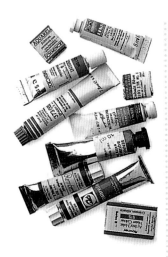

**Artists' paints**
Containing high-quality pigments, artists' paints are more expensive than students' paints but create more professional results.

# Grades of paint

There are two grades of watercolour paint: artists' (first quality) and students' (second quality). Although student-grade oil paints can be recommended for those beginners wishing to experiment without breaking the bank, student-grade watercolours are usually a false economy because they lack some of the subtlety and transparency of first-quality artists' paints.

Artist-quality paints, however, are more expensive, but they are worth the extra money, and, besides, you do not need to possess a truckload of paints in order to produce a good watercolour painting.

Having said this, the reputable paint manufacturers go to great lengths to maintain high standards at an economic price, and some artists will find students' colours perfectly acceptable for everyday

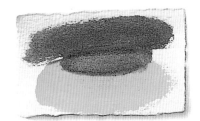

use. Certain student-grade colours may even have particular qualities which you prefer over the artists' equivalent. Thus, for example, if you want a bright green, you may find that a mixture of student-grade cobalt blue and cadmium yellow is better than the subtle green produced by the same mixture in artists' colours.

## Artists' paints

Artist-quality watercolour paints contain a high proportion of good-quality, very finely ground, permanent pigments. The colours have the advantages of being transparent and luminous as well as mixing well, and there is a wide range to choose from.

Paints are often classified by 'series', which are usually numbered from 1 to 5, according to the availability and cost of the pigments. Generally, series 5 pigments are the most costly, and series 1 the least. Go into your local art supplies store and take a look at the paint ranges on display.

**Students v. artists**
Mixing student-grade cobalt blue and cadmium yellow may give you a brighter colour than that achieved by the same mixture in artists' colours.

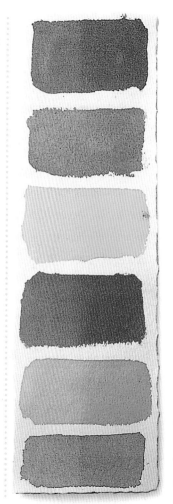

## Students' paints

Student-quality paints are usually labelled with a trade name, such as 'Cotman' (Winsor & Newton) or 'Georgian' (Daler-Rowney), and they should not be confused with the very cheap paints that are imported from the Far East and which should always be avoided.

Students' paints are sold at a uniform price, which offers the beginner an affordable yet versatile selection of colours. These paints do contain less pure pigment and more fillers and extenders than artists' paints, and many of the more expensive pigments, such as the cadmiums and cobalts, are substituted by cheaper alternatives. Such substitution is commonly indicated by the word 'hue', which is printed after the pigment name. The selection of colours available is usually smaller than that of the artists' ranges, so you may be limited to what colours you can use.

## Permanence

Watercolour is as permanent as any other medium, provided that permanent colours are used. Therefore you should always check out the manufacturer's permanency rating, which is printed either on the tube label or in their catalogue. It is also important to use acid-free paper, and to protect watercolour paintings from bright sunlight, which can cause them to fade. An interesting experiment is to paint a patch of colour onto some paper, then cover half with a piece of card and place it in bright, indirect light for several weeks. When you remove the card, you can judge the colour loss. Most good-quality paints will show little or no fading.

### Testing colour permanence
**This colour chart of student-quality watercolours was left taped to a window with half of it exposed to northern light for four months. The effects of fading can be clearly seen.**

## Transparency of colour

There are many different ways of using the unique transparency of pure watercolour, which gives a luminous glow unmatched by other painting media.

Ken Howard has captured perfectly the hazy quality of the early-morning sunlight on St Mark's Byzantine basilica in Venice (opposite left), with thin veils of shimmering colour, which have been applied in layers one over the other.

Jacqueline Rizvi (opposite right) uses watercolour mixed with Chinese white and applies translucent layers of colour very gradually, using relatively dry paint. This delicate and unusual painting technique maintains the transparent, atmospheric quality of watercolour while, at the same time, giving it a more substantial texture. This luminous study is worked on brown Japanese paper, which provides an underlying warm tone.

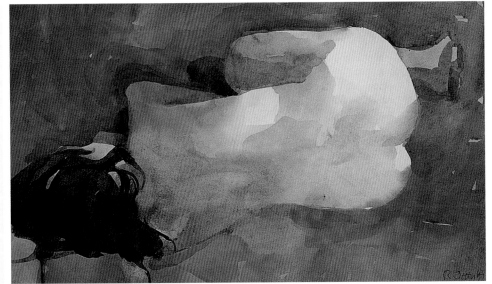

**Ronald Jesty**
*Red Nude*
**Watercolour on paper
40.5 x 51cm (16 x 20in)**

**In this study of the human form, Ronald Jesty tackles a subject which has been one of perennial fascination for artists in a subtle and luminous way.**

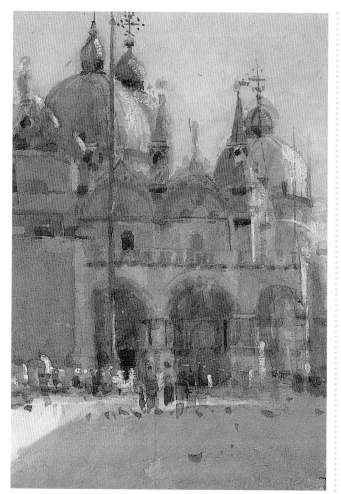

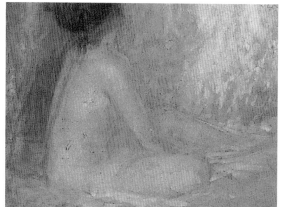

**Ken Howard**
*San Marco, Morning*
Watercolour on paper
27.5 x 22.5cm
(11 x 9in)

**Jacqueline Rizvi**
*Danae*
Watercolour on paper
27.5 x 21.2cm
(11 x 8½in)

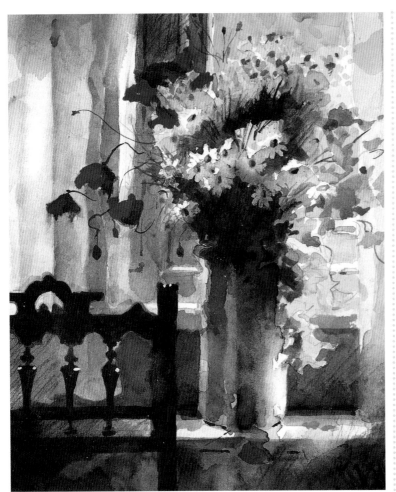

**John Lidzey**
*Wild Flowers
by the Window*
42 x 27cm
(16½ x 10½in)

**John Lidzey**
*Anna Playing
the Cello*
Watercolour on paper
66 x 45.5cm (26 x 18in)

**Alex McKibbin**
*Environs of Pamajera*
Watercolour on
paper
55 x 75cm
(22 x 30in)

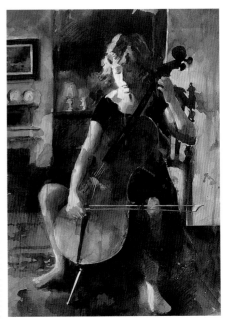

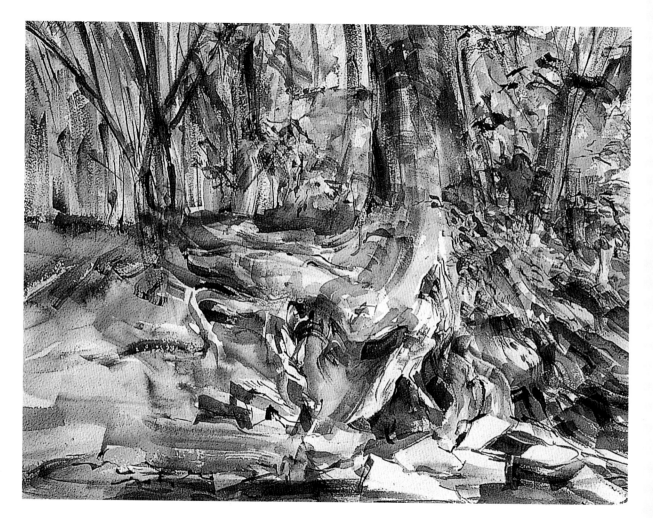

# Pigment and colour

Although watercolour is regarded as a 'transparent' medium, the pigments fall into three main groups: transparent, opaque and staining. The characteristics of each group depend on the substances from which they are derived. Additionally, some colours are intense and have greater tinting strength than others.

## Transparent pigments

Highly transparent colours permit the white reflective surface of paper to shine through. They have an attractive and airy quality, which is perfect for capturing the illusion of atmosphere, space and light. Some transparent colours are also strong stainers, although this will not concern you unless you wish to lift out certain colours.

## Opaque pigments

In watercolour, so-called 'opaque' colours are obviously far more transparent than they are in oils, particularly when they are thinly diluted. Many opaque pigments are brilliant, while others are beautifully subtle. However, these pigments impart a degree of opacity to all the colours they are mixed with – if used carelessly, they create cloudy colours lacking brilliance and luminosity.

## Staining pigments

Some transparent colours, such as alizarin crimson, are highly staining: they penetrate paper fibres and they cannot be removed

**Low-strength tints**
Colour pigments with a low tinting strength include raw umber, yellow ochre, cerulean blue and raw sienna (from top to bottom).

without leaving a trace of colour. Some earth colours, cadmiums and modern organic pigments also tend to stain; if you are intending to 'lift out' or sponge out areas of colour, you should always choose non-staining pigments where possible.

## Tinting strengths

The tinting strength of pigments varies considerably. Some are very strong and overpower in mixtures, so only a small amount is needed. However, others are so delicate that you must use a large amount in order to make an impact on another

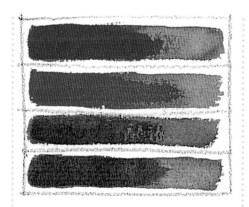

colour. Knowing how strong or weak each colour is will save you a lot of time and frustration when mixing colours together.

### Strong tints
Colours such as alizarin crimson, cadmium red, phthalocyanine blue and burnt sienna (left) are very strong, and thus they need to be diluted heavily.

### Colour characteristics
The lists below show the characteristics of some popular colours. However, brands of paint vary widely in their formulation, so test the colours yourself.

## Transparent non-staining

French ultramarine

Cobalt blue

Rose madder genuine

Aureolin

Hooker's green

Raw sienna

Payne's gray

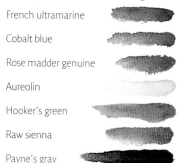

## Transparent staining

Winsor red, blue and green

Scarlet lake

Alizarin crimson

Viridian

Sap green

Prussian blue

Gamboge

## Opaque

All cadmium colours
[cadmium red shown]

Indian red

Yellow ochre

Burnt umber

Davy's grey

Cerulean blue

Lemon yellow

Raw umber

Chrome oxide green

**Cobalt blue**
**Wet paint (above) compared with a dry example (below).**

# Colour mixing

You should always mix more paint than you think you will need, as it is surprising how quickly it is used up. It is frustrating to run out of colour halfway through a wash and have to try to remix the exact colour again.

One of the keys to obtaining good colour is to restrain yourself from mixing the pigments too much. If you are blending two colours together, for example, the mixture should show three, i.e. the two original pigments as well as the mixture itself. This will give a livelier vibration to the colour.

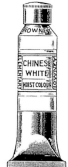

**Chinese white**
**This cool white is ideal for tinting other colours.**

Another way to ensure that you don't overmix your colours is to apply each one separately, mixing directly on the support. The colours may be applied in successive glazes (wet-on-dry), or they may be allowed to blend on dampened paper (wet-in-wet).

# Trial and error

You cannot tell just by looking at paint on a palette whether you have achieved the right colour or tone: the colour must be

**Semi-transparent colours**
**One way of using Chinese white is to dilute it and then mix it directly with transparent colours. This gives a semi-transparent, slightly milky effect, which is particularly effective on toned papers.**

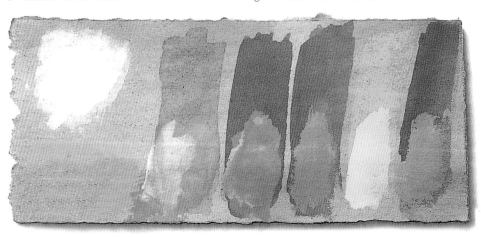

seen on paper. Watercolour paint always dries lighter on paper than it appears when wet, so mixing is often a matter of trial and error. It is useful to have a piece of spare paper to hand for testing the colours before applying them to a painting.

## Using body colour

To purists, the use of opaque paint in a watercolour is nothing short of heresy. A watercolour is supposed to be transparent, they would say, and paler tones should be achieved by adding more water to paint, while pure white areas are achieved by reserving areas of white paper. However, most watercolourists tend to take a more pragmatic approach and use opaque paint when it seems appropriate for a particular stage in a painting, as when creating highlights, for example.

Transparent watercolours can be rendered opaque or semi-opaque simply by mixing them with Chinese white to produce what is called body colour. Chinese white is a blend of zinc-oxide pigment and gum arabic; it is a dense, cool white which produces pastel tints in mixtures due to its high tinting strength.

*'One makes use of pigments, but one paints with feeling.'*
**Jean-Baptiste Chardin (1699-1779)**

---

**Mixing**
**Pigments should not be mixed too much. You should always stop mixing while you can still see the original colours along with the mixture. The lightly mixed examples (right, 2 and 3) can be seen to be more lively and colourful than the overmixed example (1).**

**1 In this example, French ultramarine and alizarin crimson have been overmixed on the palette.**

**2 Here are the same colours, but this time they are partly mixed on the palette.**

**3 The same colours again but partly mixed on some wet watercolour paper.**

25

# Basic watercolour palettes

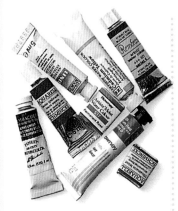

**Starter palette**
These are the only colours that you will need to get you started in watercolours.

The enormous range of colour pigments available makes it difficult to choose colours in a considered way. Who can resist those endless rows of gorgeous colours in the local art store? Of course, sets of good-quality watercolours are available in boxes, but these are expensive and they may contain far more colours than you need. A wiser course is to buy an empty box and then fill it with the colours of your own choice.

## Starter palette

The colours shown here (right) will make a suitable starting selection for beginners. Colour is a highly subjective area, but these colours have been chosen for their all-round uses and permanence. It is also possible to mix a wide range of hues from them.

**The ASTM (American Society for Testing and Materials) codes:**

ASTM I: excellent lightfastness

ASTM II: very good lightfastness

ASTM III: not sufficiently lightfast

**Cadmium yellow**
Permanence excellent (ASTM I). An opaque colour with a warm and orange-yellow hue. Very clear and bright.

**Cadmium red**
Permanence excellent (ASTM I). An opaque colour with a bright vermilion tone. Very clear and bright.

### Permanent rose
Permanence good (ASTM II). A transparent colour with a cool pinkish-red hue. A softer and more permanent alternative to alizarin crimson.

### French ultramarine
Permanence excellent (ASTM I). An excellent transparent colour with a deep blue, violet-tinged hue. Makes a range of subtle greens when mixed with yellows.

### Cobalt blue
Permanence excellent (ASTM I). A transparent colour with a soft blue hue. Cooler than French ultramarine.

### Raw sienna
Permanence excellent (ASTM I). A transparent colour, excellent for layering washes, with a deep golden-yellow hue. A very lightfast and durable colour.

### Burnt sienna
Permanence excellent (ASTM I). A transparent colour with a deep red-brown hue. Mixes well with other pigments, giving muted and subtle colours.

### Burnt umber
Permanence excellent (ASTM I). A more transparent colour than raw umber, with a warm brown hue. This is excellent in mixtures of pigments.

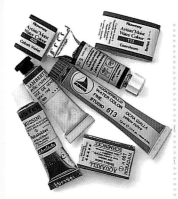

**Auxiliary palette**
These additional paints will supplement your starter palette and add colour and variety to your paintings.

# Auxiliary palette

The seven colours that are shown here (right) have been selected as a range that will extend your starter palette (see pages 26–27) for watercolour painting. Apart from the additional possibilities that they provide you with for further mixing and experimentation, you will also find that they are extremely useful when you are painting on location outdoors, particularly for creating landscapes.

## Preselected boxes

The typical shop-bought watercolour-pan box contains the colours listed below, but you can substitute or add new pans.

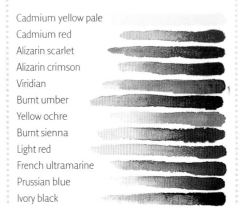

Cadmium yellow pale

Cadmium red

Alizarin scarlet

Alizarin crimson

Viridian

Burnt umber

Yellow ochre

Burnt sienna

Light red

French ultramarine

Prussian blue

Ivory black

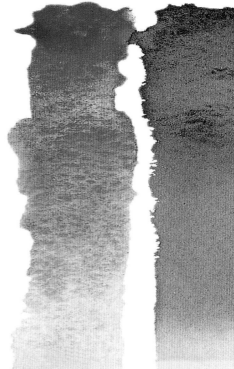

**Cerulean blue**
Permanence excellent (ASTM I). A semi-transparent colour with a cool and greenish-blue hue. Ideal for painting skies.

**Phthalocyanine blue**
Permanence good (ASTM II). A transparent colour with a deep, intense blue hue and a cold, sharp tone. A strong staining colour.

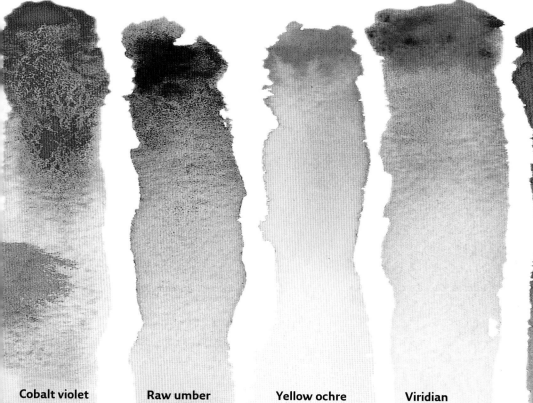

### Cobalt violet
Permanence excellent (ASTM I). A transparent colour with a bright, red-violet hue. A pure violet that cannot be mixed or imitated.

### Raw umber
Permanence excellent (ASTM I). A transparent colour with a greenish-brown hue. Useful in mixes.

### Yellow ochre
Permanence excellent (ASTM I). A transparent colour with a soft golden-yellow hue. Has a calming effect on other colours.

### Viridian
Permanence excellent (ASTM 1). A transparent colour with a cool bluish-green hue. Makes a good basis for warm, bright greens.

### Venetian red
Permanence excellent (ASTM 1). A semi-opaque colour with a warm terracotta-red hue. Very useful for mixing flesh tones.

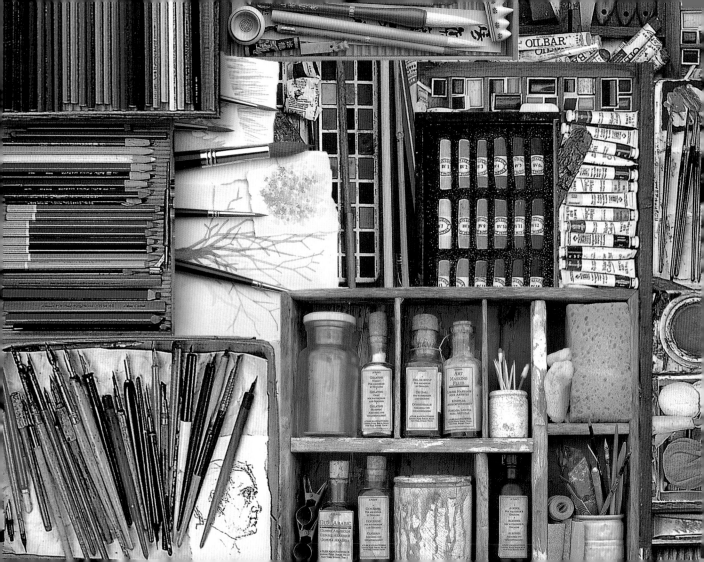

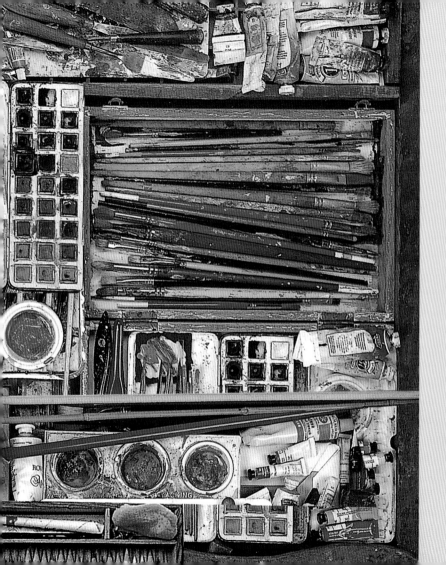

# Brushes and accessories

Brushes are a very important element in watercolour painting, so it is always worth buying the best quality that you can afford. Indeed, cheap brushes are a false economy, as they do not perform well and quickly wear out. As well as brushes, you will need to buy palettes for mixing paints and some essential accessories.

# A good brush

A good brush should have a generous 'belly', which is capable of holding plenty of colour, yet releases paint slowly and evenly. The brush should also point or edge well; when loaded with water, it should return to its original shape at the flick of the wrist.

The best brushes have a seamless ferrule made of cupro-plated nickel, which is strong and resistant to corrosion. Lower-grade brushes may have a plated ferrule with a wrapover join, but with repeated use this may tarnish or open up.

## Sable

Sable hair is obtained from the tail of the sable marten, a relative of the mink. Sable brushes are undoubtedly always the best choice for watercolour painting. They are expensive, sometimes alarmingly so, but they give the best results and, if cared for well, will last a lifetime. Sable hair tapers naturally to a fine point, so that brushes made from it have very delicate and precise tips which offer maximum control when painting details. Good-quality sable brushes are resilient yet responsive; they hold their shape well and do not shed their hairs, and have a spring and flexibility which produce lively, yet controlled brushstrokes.

**Bristles**
The bristles should point well. When loaded with water, they should return to their original shape.

**Belly**
This should hold a lot of colour, and release the paint slowly and evenly.

**Ferrule**
A seamless, cupro-plated nickel ferrule is strong and will not corrode.

**Handle**
This should be lacquered against water, chipping or cracking. Size, type and series are embossed on the handle.

12 ROWNEY S.34 SABLE 50

## Kolinsky sable

The very best sable is Kolinsky sable; it comes from the Kolinsky region of northern Siberia, where the harshness of the climate produces hair that is immensely strong, yet it is both supple and springy.

## Red sable and pure sable

Brushes marked 'red sable' or 'pure sable' are made from selected non-Kolinsky hair. They do not have the spring and shape of Kolinsky, but they are perfectly adequate and more moderately priced.

However, you should beware of buying very cheap sable brushes just because they carry the name 'sable' – good-quality sable is springy and strong, while being at the same time fine and soft.

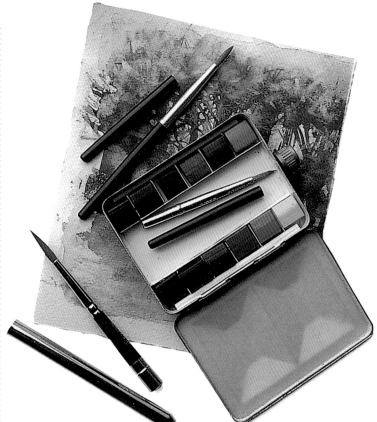

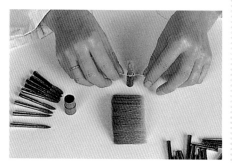

**Brush making**
Even today, brush making is largely a hand-skilled process, utilizing traditional components and natural materials.

**Portable brushes**
Small retractable brushes, with a 'travelling' set of pans, are ideal for making sketches when painting out of doors.

### Squirrel hair

This is dark brown in colour, and it is much softer than sable. Although at first sight it is much cheaper than sable, squirrel-hair brushes are generally a false economy, as they do not tend to point very well and have little resilience. Squirrel-hair 'mop' brushes, however, retain a large amount of colour, allowing extensive washes to be laid quickly and evenly. This makes them an economical alternative to large-size sable wash brushes and well worth buying.

### Ox hair

This hair comes from the ear of a breed of cow and is strong and springy, but quite coarse in texture. Although it does not point well and is not suitable for making fine-pointed brushes, it is, however, a very good hair for use in square-cut brushes.

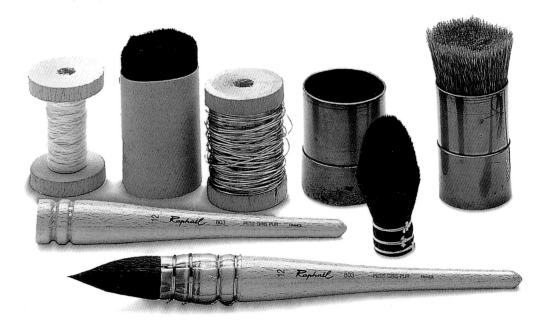

**Components and materials used in brush making**

Ox-hair brushes usually have a long hair-length, which increases their flexibility.

## Goat hair

This type of hair is often used in traditional Oriental watercolour brushes. The hair is soft but sturdy, and goat-hair brushes hold a lot of water. This makes them ideal for laying broad washes and for working wet-in-wet.

## Synthetic fibres

These brushes have been introduced in an attempt to achieve the performance of natural hair at a cheaper price. Sable-type synthetics are a golden-yellow colour and are made from polyester filaments with tapered ends, which imitate the real thing. They can be a little stiff and unsympathetic in comparison to natural hair, and have less colour-holding capacity, but synthetics in smaller sizes are a better choice for fine work than, say, squirrel hair.

## Combination brushes

Some manufacturers offer brushes that combine synthetic hair with real sable, to achieve good colour-holding and pointing properties at a reasonable cost.

**Kolinsky sable**
The best of all watercolour-brush hair: very expensive, immensely strong, yet supple and springy.

**Red or pure sable**
More moderately priced, springy and strong, yet fine and soft.

**Squirrel hair**
Softer and cheaper than sable, this does not point well and has little resilience. A less-costly alternative to large-size sable wash brushes.

**Ox hair**
Strong and springy, but quite coarse, ox hair does not point very well. Good hair for square-cut brushes.

**Goat hair**
Soft but sturdy, goat hair is ideal for laying broad washes.

**Synthetic fibres**
Synthetic fibres can be a little stiff and unsympathetic, with less colour-holding capacity than animal hair.

**Combination hair**
The brush shown is a combination of squirrel and goat hair. Other blends of animal hairs are also available, as are animal-synthetic combinations.

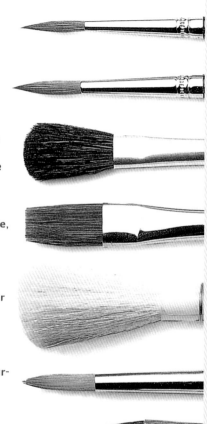

# Brush shapes and sizes

Art-supply stores and manufacturers' catalogues offer you a wide range of variations on watercolour brushes, but those detailed below will provide all you need for successful watercolour painting.

## Round brushes

The round is perhaps the most useful and most common brush shape. A brush of this type can be used for both fine, delicate strokes and broader strokes and flat washes. Apart from the standard length of brush head, rounds also come in short lengths ('spotter' brushes) and long lengths ('rigger' brushes).

## Spotter brushes

Retouching or spotter brushes have a fine point, and the very short head gives you extra control. These brushes are used mainly by miniaturists and botanical artists, for creating precise details.

## Rigger brushes

A long-haired round brush is known as a designer's point, writer or rigger (from when the brush was used for painting the finely detailed rigging on sailing ships). The long

shape gives an extra-fine point and good colour-holding properties, allowing fine lines and tapered strokes.

## Mops and wash brushes

These are made from synthetic, goat or squirrel hair, and are used for laying in large areas of colour quickly. Wash brushes are generally wide and flat, whereas mops have large round heads.

## Flat brushes

Flat watercolour brushes are also known as 'one-strokes'. These square-ended brushes, which are set into a flattened ferrule, are designed to give a high colour-carrying capacity and free flow of colour for laying in broad washes, while the chisel end creates firm, clean linear strokes. As with round brushes, a longer-haired flat is available, made from hard-wearing ox hair.

**Starter selection**
**For a good starter set of brushes, choose Nos 3, 5 and 12 round brushes.**

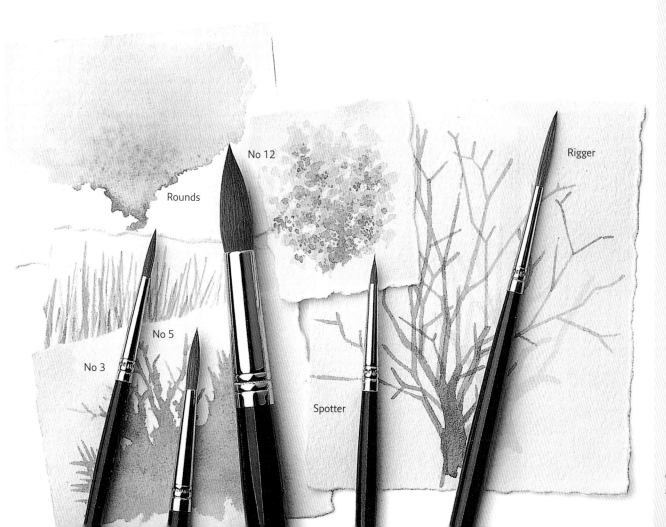

Rounds

No 12

No 5

No 3

Spotter

Rigger

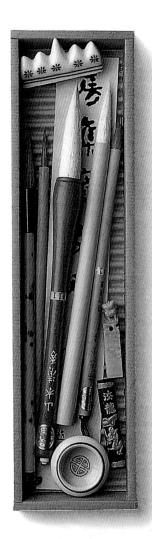

## Brush sizes

All the watercolour brushes are graded according to size, ranging from as small as 00000 to as large as a No. 24 wash brush. The size of a flat brush is generally given by its width, measured in millimetres or inches. Brush sizes are broadly similar between one manufacturer and another, but they do not appear to be standard – thus a No. 6 brush in one range will not necessarily be the same size as a No. 6 in another.

## Choosing brushes

It is a good idea to experiment with all types and sizes of brush to discover their potential. Eventually, as you develop your individual approach to watercolour, you will settle on a few brushes which are suited to

### Oriental brushes

**Oriental brushes, made from goat, wolf or hog hair set into hollow bamboo handles, are inexpensive and versatile. The thick, tapering head can make broad sweeps of colour and can be drawn up to a very fine point for painting delicate lines. The heads are coated in starch size; remove this by soaking and teasing the hairs in a jar of water for a minute or two.**

your own way of painting, and which you find comfortable to hold. To start with, a selection of three sable brushes – for instance, a No. 3, a No. 5 and a No. 12 round – should be sufficient.

As a rule, you should choose the largest suitable brush for any given application, as it is more versatile and holds more colour than a smaller version. A relatively large, good-quality brush, such as a No. 12, will cover large areas, yet come to a point fine enough to paint precise details.

## Care of brushes

• Brushes will last longer and be far more pleasant to work with if you follow a few simple rules.

• While painting, do not leave brushes resting on their bristles in water for long periods, as this can ruin the hairs and handles.

• Immediately after use, rinse brushes in cold running water, making sure that any paint near the ferrule is fully removed.

• After cleaning, shake out the excess water and gently shape up the hairs between finger and thumb. A little starch solution or thinned gum solution stroked onto the bristles will help them retain their shape; it is easily rinsed out with water when the brush is used again.

• Leave your brushes to dry either flat or up-ended in a pot or jar. When storing brushes for any length of time, make sure they are perfectly dry before placing them in a box that has a tight-fitting lid – mildew may develop if wet brushes are stored in an airtight container.

• Moths are partial to animal-hair bristles, so protect your brushes in the long term with mothballs or a sachet of camphor. Horse chestnuts also keep moths at bay.

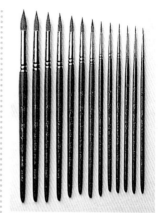

**Sable rounds**
**The brushes shown here range from 000 up to 12; even smaller and larger brushes are available.**

Flats

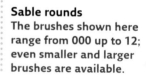

Orientals

Mop brush

# Palettes

Watercolour palettes are now available in a variety of shapes and sizes. However, they all feature recesses or wells which allow you to add the required quantity of water to the paint. These recesses also prevent separate colours from running together.

## Choosing a palette

Manufactured palettes are usually made of white ceramic, enamelled metal or plastic; of these materials, ceramic is perhaps the most sympathetic surface for mixing your colours. Basic plastic palettes have the advantage of being cheap and lightweight as well as being ideal for outdoor painting. However, they will eventually become stained with paint residue because they are slightly absorbent and will need to be replaced. Which kind of palette you prefer to use will be largely dependent on your personal taste and the scale and style of your work. However, as we shall see, certain types of palette are best suited to particular purposes, so it is worth getting the right one.

**Types of palettes**
**Quartered ceramic tinting saucer (top) and round cabinet saucers (bottom).**

## Integral palettes

Enamelled-metal painting boxes, designed to hold pans or tubes of paint, are useful when working outdoors, as the inside of the lid doubles as a palette and mixing area when opened out. Some boxes also have an integral hinged flap for mixing and tinting, and a thumb ring in the base.

## Slanted-well tiles

These are long ceramic palettes divided into several recesses or wells, allowing several colours to be laid out without them flowing into one another. The wells slant, so the paint collects at one end ready for use and can be drawn out for thinner washes. Some slanted-well tiles have a

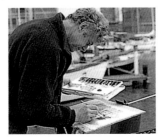

row of smaller and a row of larger wells; paint is squeezed into the small wells and moved to the larger wells, to be diluted with water or mixed with other colours.

## Tinting saucers

These small round ceramic dishes are used for mixing larger quantities of paint. They are available divided into four recesses, for mixing separate colours, or they may be undivided, for mixing a single colour.

## Palette trays

When you are mixing large quantities of liquid paint, you will need to use a palette with deep wells. These palettes are usually made of plastic or more stain-resistant, high-impact polystyrene.

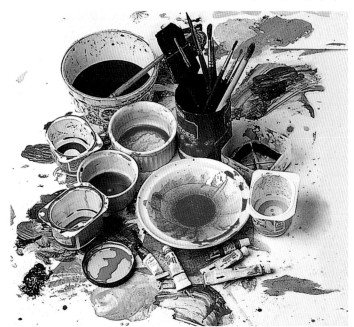

### Improvised palettes

**Improvised palettes are cheap and easy to obtain, and artists often prefer them because there is no restriction on size. You can use a variety of household containers, as long as they are white and non-porous. Depending on how large a mixing area you want, use a white saucer, plate or enamelled pie plate. Hors-d'oeuvres dishes are useful, as they provide several large mixing areas. When you are mixing large quantities of wash, use old cups, bowls or yoghurt pots.**

**Palettes for watercolour**
Shown here and on the opposite page are a selection of manufactured palettes which are suitable for watercolour painting. Right: deep-well palette tray (top); and large plastic mixing palette with thumb hole and divisions (bottom). Opposite: enamelled-metal painting box with integral palette (top left); ceramic slanted-well tile (top right); segmented white china round palette (bottom right); and plastic mixing palette (bottom left).

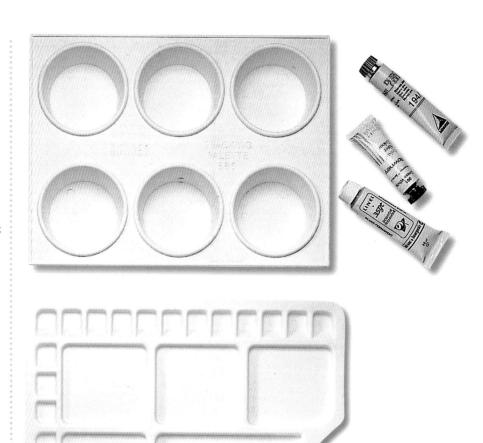

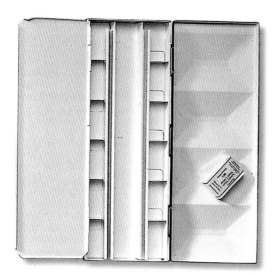

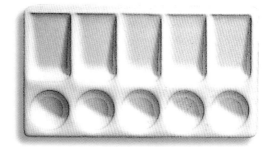

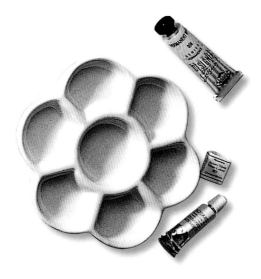

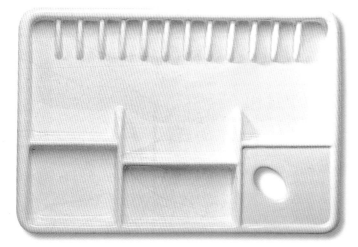

# Watercolour accessories

Some useful accessories and items, such as water containers, mediums, masking fluid, scraping tools and sponges, will all help to broaden the range of painting techniques at your disposal.

## Water containers

Do not skimp on water when you are painting in watercolour. Use as large a container as you can find; otherwise the water quickly becomes murky as you rinse your brush between washes, and this may well spoil the transparency of your finished colours. Some artists prefer to use two water containers – one for rinsing their brushes and the other to use as a dipper for mixing colours.

## Masking fluid

This is a quick-drying, liquid latex which can be used to mask off selected areas of a painting when applying colour in broad washes. There are two types available: tinted and colourless. The tinted version is preferable, as it is more versatile and is easier to work with on white paper.

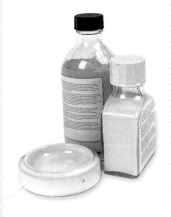

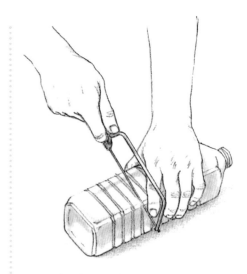

**Improvised containers**
You can recycle plastic bottles into useful water containers – some bottles have convenient guidelines for cutting. Cut to the required height with either a hacksaw or craft knife; the leftover neck can be used as a funnel.

## Gum arabic

A pale-coloured solution of gum arabic in water will increase both the gloss and transparency of watercolour paints when it is mixed with them. Diluted further, it improves paint flow. Be careful not to use too much gum arabic as it will make paint slippery and jelly-like. However, when used in moderation it enlivens the texture and enhances the vividness of the colours.

## Ox gall

Ox gall is a straw-coloured liquid made from the gallbladders of cattle, which is added to water in jars to improve both the flow and adhesion of watercolour paints, particularly for wet-in-wet techniques. Nowadays, it has been largely replaced by synthetic products.

## Gelatine size

This liquid, which is sold in small bottles, may be applied to the surface of any watercolour paper which is too absorbent. Apply the gelatine size with a large soft brush, and leave to dry for a few minutes. The size reduces the absorbency of paper, making it easier to apply washes.

## Glycerine

You will find glycerine particularly useful when you are working on location outdoors in dry conditions. A few drops of glycerine added to some water will counteract the drying effects of the wind and hot sun by prolonging the time that it takes for the watercolour paint to dry naturally.

## Alcohol

This actually has the opposite effect to that of glycerine – which is described above – speeding up the drying time of watercolour paint. Again, alcohol is extremely useful when working outdoors but in damp weather conditions rather than dry ones.

## Distilled water

The majority of artists use ordinary tap water, but some watercolour painters prefer to use distilled water for mixing their colours, as it contains no impurities and can discourage granulation (see page 108). When painting, don't skimp on water. Always use as large a container as is

**Painting outdoors**
If painting outdoors, use a plastic water container, which is lighter and less liable to break than glass. You can buy collapsible plastic containers with a handle, or simply cut the top off a plastic bottle. You may also have to transport water to your location, and a larger container to decant from will be useful.

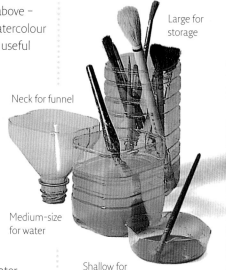

Large for storage

Neck for funnel

Medium-size for water

Shallow for mixing

practicable. If the container is too small, the water becomes murky from washing out your brushes and it may even spoil the transparency of your colours.

## Scraping and lifting tools

You can use a single-edged razor blade, scalpel, cocktail stick, end of a paintbrush handle or even your thumbnail for scraping out unwanted areas of still-wet watercolour or scratching lines into dry paint to create textured effects. Fine sandpaper can be used to rub away some of the colour, creating a drybrush-like sparkle. Cotton buds can be used for lifting out small areas of still-wet colour. Blotting paper is also useful for lifting out colour and mopping up spills.

## Sponges

Natural and synthetic sponges are used for dabbing on areas of rough-textured paint. They are also used for wetting paper in preparation for applying washes, and to lift out wet paint or mop up paint that has run too much. Natural sponges are more expensive than synthetic ones but they have a pleasing silky texture and produce some interesting random patterns.

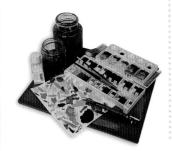

## Mahlstick

This has a long handle with a pad at one end. It is used to steady the painting arm when executing detailed, controlled work. You can improvise your own by tightly wrapping cotton wool into a ball around the end of a garden cane. Cover with a disc of cloth or chamois leather, larger than the ball, and secure with elastic bands.

## Stool

A small canvas folding stool is light enough to carry when painting outdoors. If you prefer to work standing up, use it to hold your palette, brushes and so on.

**Selection of accessories**
**Shown opposite is a typical assortment of materials used to create watercolour textures and expand techniques. Top shelf, from left to right: water container for mixing and wetting; gelatine; ox gall; masking fluid; cotton buds and cocktail sticks; natural and synthetic sponges. Bottom shelf, from left to right: clips for holding paper; gum arabic; glycerine; water container for washing brushes; alcohol abrasive paper; craft knives and sharpened paintbrushes for lifting and scraping.**

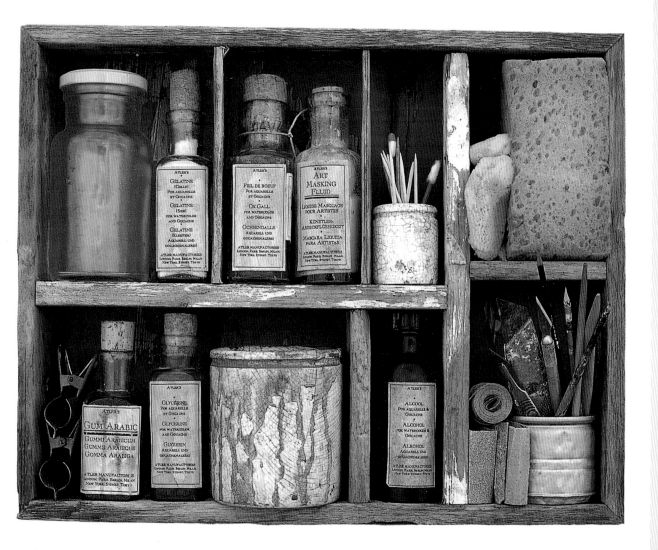

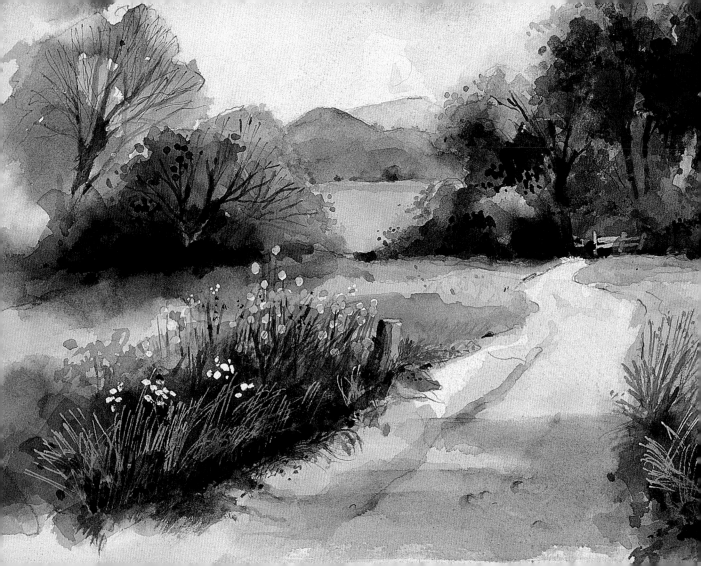

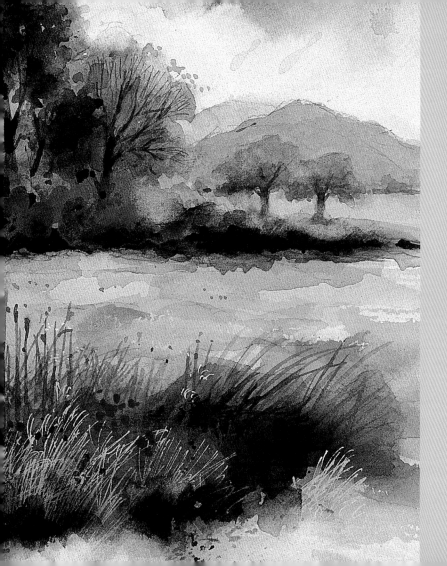

# Watercolour papers

A well-known professor of painting used to say that no artist really succeeds until he has found his ideal paper. Today there are plenty of excellent watercolour papers on the market to choose from, and it is well worth experimenting in order to find the one that best responds to your working method.

**John Lidzey**
*Suffolk Landscape*
Watercolour on paper
33 x 51cm (13 x 20in)

# Paper production

There are three different ways of producing watercolour paper: by hand; on a mould machine; and on a fourdrinier machine.

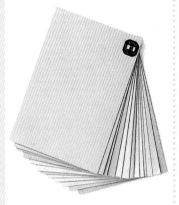

**Try before you buy**
Trial-and-error can be a costly affair, given the price of the average sheet of watercolour paper. However, most paper manufacturers produce swatches or pochettes – booklets containing small samples of their ranges. These provide an excellent and inexpensive means of trying out several different types of paper.

### Handmade paper

The very best papers are made of 100 per cent cotton, usually by skilled craftsmen. Handmade papers are lively to use, durable, and have a pleasing irregular texture. They are expensive, but worth the cost.

### Mould-made paper

European mills produce watercolour paper on cylinder-mould machines. The paper fibres are formed into sheets with a random distribution, which is close to that of handmade papers. The paper is durable, extremely stable, and resistant to distortion under a heavy wash.

### Machine-made paper

Although inexpensive to produce and to purchase, machine-made papers are less resistant to deterioration, but they may distort when wet. Some papers also have a mechanical, monotonous surface grain.

### Choosing paper

Watercolour paper is an excellent surface for acrylics, pencil, ink, gouache and pastel, as well as watercolour. The character of the paper, and its surface texture, play a vital role in the finished picture. Very often it is the choice of paper that is to blame for a painting going wrong, rather than any inadequacy on the part of the artist.

**Texture**
There are three different textures of watercolour paper: (from left to right) rough, Not or cold-pressed (medium grain), and hot-pressed or HP (smooth). Each manufacturer's range is likely to have a slightly different feel.

Some papers are superior in quality to others, but it does not necessarily follow that an expensive paper will give you better results. The important thing is to find a paper that is sympathetic to what you want to do. For example, it is no good using an absorbent rag paper if your watercolour technique involves repeated scrubbing, lifting out and using masking fluid – the surface will soon become woolly and bruised.

## Sourcing papers

Popular papers are available in your local art shops. Specialist art shops stock less-common and handmade or foreign papers; some of these are also available either by mail-order direct from the mill or though distributors, who can send you sample swatches, price lists and order forms. Once you have settled on your favourite paper, it pays to buy in quantity. The bigger the order, the more you save.

## Experimenting with watercolour papers

Try out different textures and makes of watercolour paper until you find one which suits your painting style. As you become more knowledgeable, you will also be able to choose a paper to suit your subject.

### Hot-pressed paper

Hot-pressed paper has a hard, smooth surface that is suitable for detailed, precise work. Most artists, however, find this surface too smooth and slippery, and the paint tends to run out of control.

### Cold-pressed paper

This is also referred to as 'Not', meaning not hot-pressed. It has a semi-rough surface equally good for smooth washes and fine brush detail. This is the most popular and versatile of the three surfaces, and it is ideal for less-experienced painters. It responds well to washes, and has enough texture to give a lively finish.

### Rough paper

This has a more pronounced tooth (tiny peaks and hollows) to its surface. When a colour wash is laid on it, the brush drags over the surface and the paint settles in some of the hollows, leaving others untouched. This leaves a sparkle of white to illuminate the wash.

51

**Smooth-texture paper**

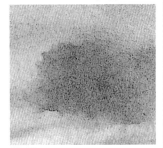

**Medium-texture paper**

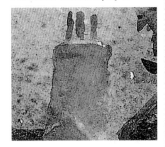

**Rough-texture paper**

In the examples below and opposite, the artist has chosen a smooth texture for the nude study, which is perfectly appropriate for the tone and texture of the flesh. The winter-evening snow scene is ideally suited for a medium-texture paper which conveys the effect of misty light and captures the subtle grain of the snow. A rough-texture paper (below) helps to communicate the solidity of the building and the dampness of the weather to the viewer.

**Trevor Chamberlain**
*Late-evening Effect Showery Evening, Isleworth* (below); *Reclining Nude* (opposite top); and *Snow* (bottom).
**All watercolour on paper**
**Various dimensions**

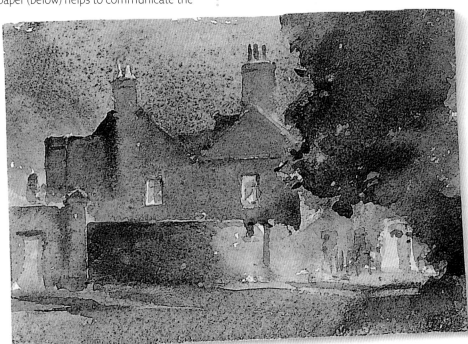

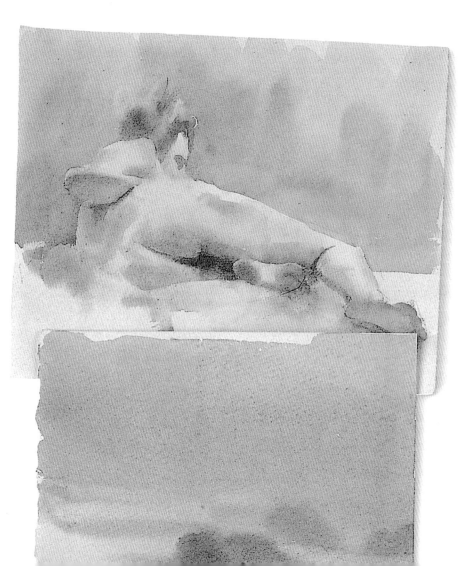

## Paper sizes

Sizes of papers will differ from country to country, and it is still common practice for art suppliers to describe paper in imperial sizes. The following table is a guide to imperial sizes and their metric equivalents.

**Medium**
22 x 17½in
(559 x 444mm)

**Royal**
24 x 19in
(610 x 483mm)

**Double Crown**
30 x 20in
(762 x 508mm)

**Imperial**
30½ x 22½in
(775 x 572mm)

**Double Elephant**
40 x 26¼in
(1016 x 679mm)

**Antiquarian**
53 x 31in
(1346 x 787mm)

# Choosing watercolour papers

Choice of watercolour papers is very much a matter of personal preference; one artist's favourite may be another artist's poison. The chart below is intended only as a guide to a versatile selection of widely available papers. They have all been tried and tested by professional watercolour artists; however, your own assessment may be quite different.

### Esportazione by Fabriano
Handmade paper
Surfaces: Not and rough
Weights: 200, 315, 600gsm Content: 100% cotton rag, tub-sized

A robust, textured surface that stands up to erasure and scrubbing, carries washes without sinking. Four deckle edges. Watermarked.

### Richard de Bas by Richard de Bas
Handmade paper
Surfaces: HP, Not and rough Weight: 480gsm Content: 100% cotton rag, internally sized

A thick, robust paper with a fibrous texture. Washes fuse into the paper structure. Four deckle edges. Watermarked.

### Indian by Khadi
Handmade paper
Surfaces: HP and Not
Weights: 200 and 300gsm Content: 100% cotton rag, internally sized

A strong paper, which is able to withstand plenty of wear and tear. Lifting out colour is easy, and masking fluid rubs off well on this paper.

### Artists' Paper by Two Rivers
Handmade paper
Surface: Not
Weights: 175, 250gsm Content: 100% cotton rag, tub-sized, loft-dried; buffered with calcium carbonate

Gently absorbent, but robust and firm. Also available in cream, oatmeal and grey. Four deckle edges.

**Arches Aquarelle
by Canson**
Mould-made paper
Surfaces: HP, Not and
rough Weights: 185, 300,
640, 850gsm
Content: 100% cotton rag,
tub-sized, air-dried

A warm white paper.
Carries washes without
undue absorption. Resists
scrubbing and scratching.
Lifting out is difficult,
and fibre-lift occurs when
masking fluid is removed.

**Lana Aquarelle
by Lana**
Mould-made paper
Surfaces: HP, Not and
rough Weights: 185, 300,
600gsm Content: 100%
cotton rag, tub-sized

A good, textured surface.
Lifting out and removal
of masking fluid are easy.
All weights stand up well
to washes without undue
buckling.

**Bockingford
by Inveresk**
Mould-made paper
Surface: Not
Weights: 190, 300, 425,
535gsm
Content: 100% cotton rag,
internally sized, buffered
with calcium carbonate

A versatile, economical
paper, Robust yet gently
absorbent. Lifting out is
easy; masking fluid comes
away cleanly. 300gsm is
also available in tints.

**Saunders Waterford
by St Cuthbert's Mill**
Mould-made paper
Surfaces: HP, Not and
rough Weights: 190, 300,
356, 640gsm
Content: 100% cotton rag,
internally and gelatine
sized

A stable, firm paper,
which is resistant to
cockling, and with a
sympathetic surface.
Scrubbing, lifting out
and masking are easy.

*'First of all, respect your paper!'*
**J. M. W. Turner (1775–1851),
on being asked for his
advice about painting**

## Paper content

Apart from water, the main ingredient in making paper is cellulose fibres, derived from either cotton or woodpulp. Cotton is used for high-grade papers, woodpulp for others. Some papers contain a blend of cotton and other cellulose fibres, offering a compromise between cost and quality.

### Cotton rag

The best paper is made from 100 per cent cotton. Although the term 'rag paper' is still used, the raw material nowadays is natural cotton linters. Rag papers are very strong, yet pliable, and withstand demanding techniques.

### Woodpulp

Woodpulp produces a more economical, but less durable, paper. Confusingly, papers made of 100 per cent woodpulp are sometimes advertised as 'woodfree'; this is a technical term meaning wood broken down by chemical means, rather than mechanical ones – it does not signify that the paper has not been made from wood. Mechanical woodpulp still contains lignin, which releases acids into the paper over a period of time, causing it to yellow and embrittle. The chemical woodpulp that is used in woodfree paper is processed to remove all the lignin.

## Weight

The weight (thickness) of watercolour paper traditionally refers to the weight of a ream (500 sheets) of a given size, most often imperial (about 22 x 30in or 56 x 76cm). For instance, a 72lb paper is a light paper, 500 sheets of which weigh 72lb. The more accurate metric equivalent of grammes per square metre (gsm) is now common. Lighter papers (less than 300gsm/140lb) tend to buckle and wrinkle when washes are applied, and they will need wetting and stretching on a board before use. Heavier grades don't need to be stretched unless you intend to flood the paper with washes.

**Weights of watercolour paper**

| Metric | Imperial |
| --- | --- |
| 150gsm | 72lb |
| 180gsm | 90lb |
| 300gsm | 140lb |
| 410gsm | 200lb |
| 600gsm | 300lb |
| 850gsm | 400lb |

# Absorbency and sizing

All watercolour paper is internally sized to varying degrees, to control its absorbency and produce a more receptive working surface. Heavy sizing produces a hard surface with little absorption and a long drying time; this allows you to push the paint around on the surface. Colours remain brilliant, as they are not dulled by sinking into the paper. Lightly sized papers are softer and more absorbent, with a shorter drying time. Alterations are more difficult as the paint sinks into the fibres of the paper, but absorbent papers are suited to direct, expressive painting methods.

## Internal sizing

Internal, or 'engine' sizing means that size is added to the paper at the pulp stage, and contained in the body of the paper. Internal sizing renders the paper robust and prevents colour washes cross-bleeding beneath the paper surface, even when it has been abraded.

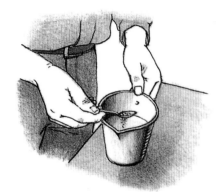

**Increasing sizing**
If paper is too absorbent, paint sinks into it and the colours appear dull. To remedy this, dissolve a teaspoon of gelatin granules in half a litre (1.1 pints) of water and then apply to the surface of the paper before painting.

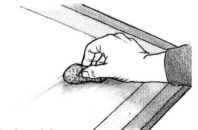

**Reducing sizing**
If a heavily sized paper does not take paint well, then pass a damp sponge over the surface several times. Leave it for 30 minutes, then dampen again before painting. Some handmade papers may need to be soaked for up to two hours in some warm water.

## Acid content
**Papers that contain an acid presence, such as newsprint and brown wrapping paper, are prone, in time, to yellowing and deterioration. Paper acidity is measured by the pH scale. An acid-free paper does not contain any chemicals which might cause degradation of the sheet, and will normally have a pH of around 7 (neutral). All good-quality watercolour papers are acid-free, in order to prevent embrittlement and yellowing with age. Some are also buffered with calcium carbonate, to protect against acids in the atmosphere.**

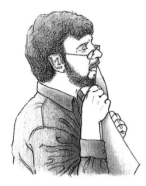

**Trying for size**
**The amount and quality of sizing varies according to the brand of paper. A quick test is to lick a corner of the paper with the end of your tongue: if it feels dry and sticks to your tongue, you will know that it is absorbent paper.**

## Surface sizing

Many watercolour papers are also surface-sized, which is done by being passed through a tub of gelatin size (hence the term 'tub-sized'). Surface sizing not only reduces the absorbency of the paper but it also produces a more luminous wash (on absorbent papers, colours tend to dry far paler than they appear as a wet wash). It also reduces the risk of fibre lift when you are removing masking material and lifting out washes of colour.

## Tinted papers

Most watercolour paper is either white or off-white, to reflect the maximum amount of light back through the transparent washes of colour. Some manufacturers,

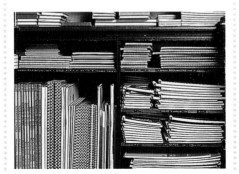

however, specialize in a range of tinted papers, and these are often used when painting with body colour or gouache.

You should always check that the tinted paper you buy is sufficiently lightfast. Good-quality papers will not fade under normal conditions, but cheaper paper may not be as permanent as the colours that are laid on it, and in time the change could affect the overall tone of your painting. Many artists prefer to apply their own tint by laying a very thin wash on white paper.

## Watercolour sheets

Watercolour paper is most commonly sold in sheet form. In addition, many mills supply their papers in rolls, which are more economical, and pads. Spiral-bound pads are particularly useful for when you are working outdoors. They are available in a wide range of sizes, although they usually contain 300gsm (140lb) Not paper.

### Spiral pads
**Watercolour paper can also be bought in the form of spiral-bound pads, which are convenient for outdoor sketching. These pads generally contain 300gsm (140lb) Not paper.**

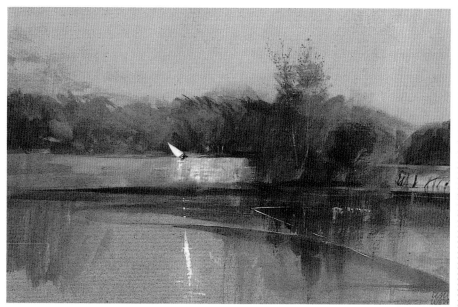

**Leslie Worth**
*Windsurfer on Boldermere*
**Watercolour on brown paper**
**22.5 x 28.7cm (9 x 11½in)**

Though a tiny shape, the windsurf board is very much the focal point of this picture. Surrounded by dark tones and neutral colours, the sharp accent of the white sail sings out with a piercing note on the brown watercolour paper.

## Watercolour blocks

These comprise sheets of watercolour paper which are 'glued' together round the edges with gum. This block of paper is mounted on a backing board. A watercolour block removes the need for stretching paper. When the painting is completed, the top sheet is removed by sliding a palette knife between the top sheet and the one below. Although more expensive than loose sheets, watercolour blocks are both convenient and time-saving for artists.

## Watercolour boards

Watercolour board is yet another way of avoiding the use of stretching paper. It consists of watercolour paper which is mounted onto a strong backing board in order to improve its performance with heavy washes.

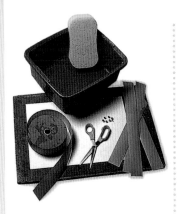

**The best equipment**
Use only gummed brown-paper tape for stretching paper – masking tape and self-adhesive tape will not adhere to damp paper. A clean wooden drawing board is the ideal surface for stretching paper; traces of paint or ink might stain the paper. Plastic-coated boards are not suitable, because gummed tape will not stick to them.

# Stretching paper

Wet paint causes the fibres in watercolour paper to swell, and this can lead to buckling, or 'cockling' of the surface. To prevent this happening, you should stretch paper before starting to work on it.

## Achieving a smooth painting surface

The paper is wetted and then securely taped to a board. On drying, it will contract slightly and become taut, giving a smooth surface that is less prone to cockling. With heavier papers (300gsm and over) there is less need for stretching, unless heavy, saturated washes are to be applied. Lighter papers always need stretching.

## Method

Cut four lengths of gummed brown-paper tape 50mm (2in) longer than the paper. Always do this first, to avoid any panic at the crucial moment, when wet hands, crumpled tape and a rapidly curling sheet of paper could cause chaos.

Immerse the paper in cold water for a few minutes, making sure that it has absorbed water on both sides – heavier

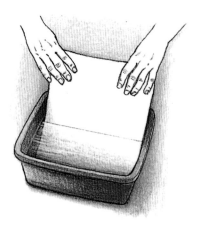

**Immersing the paper**

papers may take up to 20 minutes. Use a container large enough to take the sheet without being cramped. For large sheets, you can use a clean sink or bath.

Immerse only one sheet of paper at a time in fresh water, as each sheet will leave a residue of size in the water.

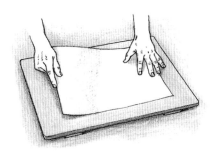

**Smoothing the paper**

Hold the paper up by one corner and then shake it gently to drain the surplus water. Place the paper on the board and smooth it out from the centre, using your hands, to make sure that it is perfectly flat.

Take a dry sponge around the edges of the paper where the gummed tape is to be placed, to remove any excess water. You

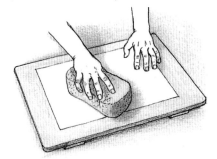

**Removing excess water**

should moisten each length of gum strip with a damp sponge immediately before use. Beginning with the long sides, stick the strips around the outer edges of the paper, half their width on the board, half on the paper.

Leave the paper to dry flat, allowing it to dry naturally, away from direct heat. Do not attempt to use stretched paper until it is dry. Leave the gummed strips in place until the painting is completed and dry.

## Commercial paper stretchers

For those artists who find stretching paper a time-consuming chore, the only previous alternative to this process has been to use expensive heavyweight papers or boards. However, there are now various effective devices available, which are designed by watercolour painters and which will stretch lightweight papers drum-tight in minutes. Among the ingenious designs, one uses a two-piece wooden frame to hold the paper firmly in place as it dries; another employs a system of plastic gripper rods which are pushed into grooves in the edges of the board, to hold the paper.

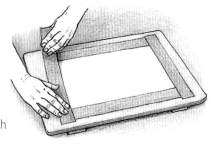

**Sticking the gummed strip**

**Immersion times**
**These depend on the weight and degree of surface sizing of the paper. Thin paper soaked for too long will expand greatly, and may tear as it contracts; too brief an immersion means the paper will not expand enough and will buckle when wet paint is applied. The correct soaking time for each paper will come through trial and error, but in general lightweight papers and those not strongly sized should be soaked for 2-3 minutes; heavily sized papers may need 5-10 minutes. (If a fine layer of bubbles appears, this indicates a strongly sized paper.)**

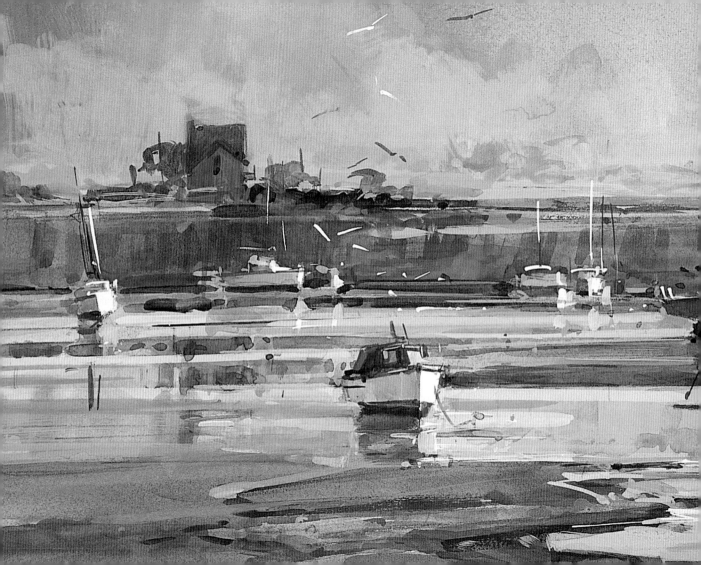

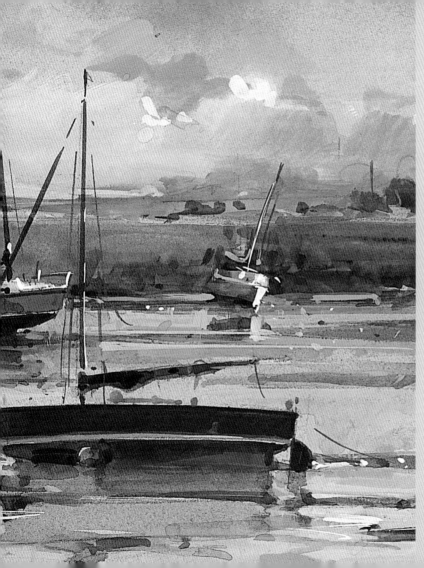

# Other water-based media

Many artists choose to work in other water-based media, most notably gouache, egg tempera and water-soluble colour pencils. More opaque and less luminous than watercolours, gouache creates a more solid and robust finish yet retains a brilliant light-reflecting quality. The more traditional tempera paints suit those artists with a detailed and meticulous approach to their work.

**Ray Balkwill**
*Evening Sky, Topsham (detail)*
Watercolour and gouache
25 x 36cm (10 x 14in)

# Gouache

The term 'gouache' originates from the Renaissance, when the Italian masters painted *a gouazzo* – with water-based distemper or size paints. The opacity of gouache and its matt, chalky appearance when dry, make it a quite separate and distinct medium from pure, transparent watercolour, but the equipment, supports and techniques that are used are similar for both media.

## Paints

The best-quality gouache paints contain a very high proportion of pigment; its density creates an opaque effect. The colours are therefore pure and intense, and they create clean colour mixes. Because the natural covering power of each pigment is not increased artificially, it varies according to the pigment. The less-expensive gouache ranges contain an inert white pigment, such as chalk or blanc fixe, to impart smoothness and opacity.

## Availability of gouache

Standard-size tubes are very convenient when you are painting outdoors, but pots of gouache are more economical for executing large-scale paintings.

**Testing gouache**
In terms of permanence, covering power and flow, gouache colours will vary considerably from one manufacturer to another, and it is advisable to try out samples from different ranges to determine which are best suited to your own method of working.

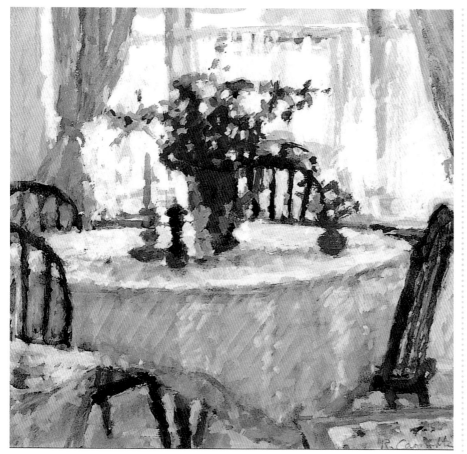

**Rosemary Carruthers**
*Window Table*
*(The Moorings)*
Gouache on paper
21.2 x 23.7cm (8½ x 9½in)
Llewellyn Alexander
Gallery, London

Depending on your
temperament as an artist,
you can choose either to
exploit the brilliance and
opacity of gouache or to
create soft, subtle effects.
This interior study (left)
evokes a quiet, reflective
mood. Here, the artist
has used overlaid washes
of semi-opaque colour,
softened with white.
The matt and airy quality
of the paint surface
beautifully recreates the
suffused light on the scene.

## Choosing paint

Gouache paints are often labelled 'designers' colour' due to their popularity with graphic designers, who need bright colours with a matt finish. The vast range of colours includes some brilliant colours which are fugitive. This does not matter to designers, but these colours are not recommended for fine permanent painting.

## Colour migration

Certain dye-based gouache colours – the lakes, magentas and violets – have a tendency to 'migrate', or bleed through when overpainted with light colours. One solution is to apply bleed-proof white between the layers, to halt any further migration. This is a very dense designers' colour that may be classed as gouache.

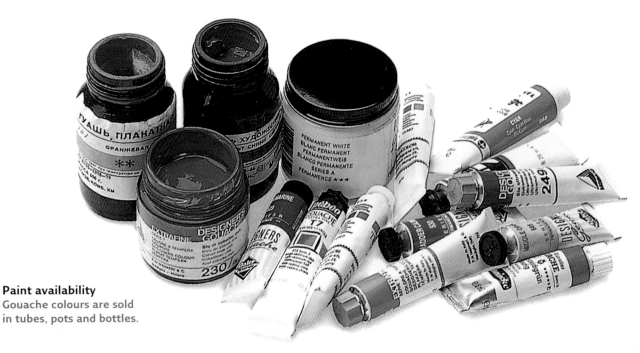

**Paint availability**
Gouache colours are sold in tubes, pots and bottles.

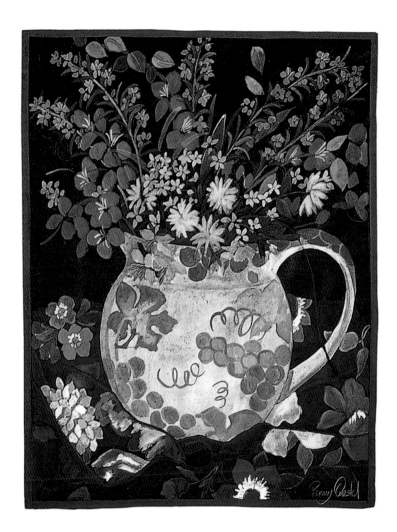

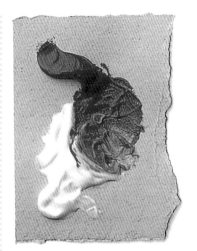

**Preventing colour migration**
Colours may be mixed with acrylic glaze medium, which converts gouache into paint with an acrylic finish that is both flexible and water-resistant. It allows washes to be superimposed without disturbing those below.

**Penny Quested**
*Still Life with Flowers*
Gouache on Japanese paper
67.5 x 57.5cm (27 x 23in)

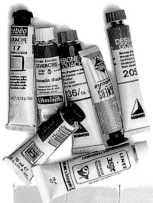

## Basic gouache palette

As with the basic watercolour palette, the selection of colours below will enable you to discover the basic characteristics of gouache paints. The basic selection may then be augmented with further colours from the wide range available, depending on the subjects that you wish to paint.

## Starting selection

All manufactured gouache colours are opaque and they have a high degree of permanence. Colours can be intermixed and thinned with water (below left) to create transparent colours which look similar to true watercolour paint, or mixed with white paint (below) for opaque tints.

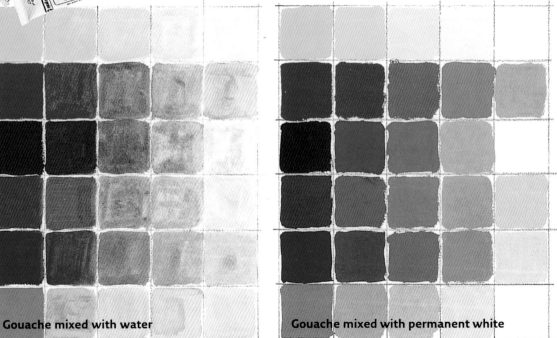

**Gouache mixed with water**

**Gouache mixed with permanent white**

## Starting selection (opposite from top to bottom)

### Cadmium yellow
Permanence excellent (ASTM I).
Lemon shades through to warm orange.
Mixes well, forming strong greens when mixed with viridian.

### Cadmium red
Permanence excellent (ASTM I).
Warm orange-red to deep red. A strong, pure pigment, which is excellent in mixes.

### French ultramarine
Permanence excellent (ASTM I).
Deep blue with a slightly violet tinge.
When mixed with yellows, it provides a useful, versatile range of greens.

### Raw umber
Permanence excellent (ASTM I).
Brown with a slightly greenish-brown tinge.
Raw umber is particularly good for neutralizing other colours.

### Viridian
Permanence excellent (ASTM I).
Cool, bluish green. Retains its brilliance, even in mixes.

### Yellow ochre
Permanence excellent (ASTM I). Soft, golden yellow. Tones down brighter colours in mixes.

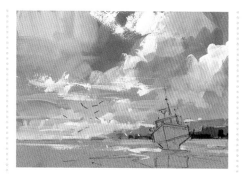

## Supports
Since gouache is opaque, the translucency of white paper is not as vital as it is when you are using watercolour, so it can be applied to a wide variety of supports.
Lightweight papers should be avoided; the paint film of gouache is thicker than that of watercolour, and is liable to crack if used on a too-flimsy support. Gouache can also be used on surfaces such as cardboard, wood or primed canvas, so long as they are free

**The ASTM (American Society for Testing and Materials) codes for lightfastness:**
ASTM I: excellent lightfastness
ASTM II: very good lightfastness
ASTM III: not sufficiently lightfast

**Ray Balkwill**
*Weather Conditions*
**Gouache on paper**
**14 x 19cm (5½ x 7½in)**

Windy weather is difficult to convey in any medium. You usually have to rely on devices such as trees bent in the wind or a flurry of leaves. In this painting horizontal strokes made with a dry brush convey a sense of movement in clouds that scud across an energetic sky. Also, birds can be seen battling with the strong wind.

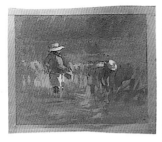

**John Martin**
*Untitled Sketch*
**Gouache on tinted paper**
**10 x 15cm (4 x 6in)**

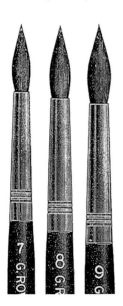

from oil. You can also employ toned and coloured papers, as used for pastel work.

## Brushes

Watercolour brushes are normally used for gouache painting, although bristle brushes can be useful for making textural marks. However, because gouache does not handle in the same way as watercolour, experiment to determine which type and size of brush best suits your technique.

**Edward McKnight Kauffer (1890–1954)**
*Untitled Litho Print, 1919*
**75 x 112cm (30 x 44¾in)**
**Museum of Modern Art, New York**

**Posters were traditionally painted on board or stretched paper with gouache, tempera or cheap and impermanent 'poster colours'. Gouache colours were the first choice of graphic designers and commercial artists for many years. Their strong colour and solid, velvety, non-reflective surface finish photograph well, enabling artwork to be converted accurately to print.**

## Using toned paper

Toned paper can be highly effective when working with gouache; the surface acts as a mid-tone from which to work up to the lights and down to the darks, and also helps to unify the elements of the composition (see the sketch, left). If you intend leaving some areas of the paper untouched, however, do make sure that you always choose a good-quality paper which will not fade with the passage of time.

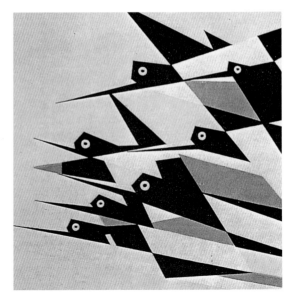

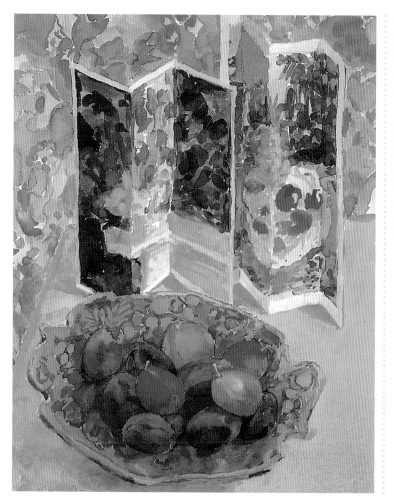

**Geraldine Girvan**
*Plums in a Green Dish*
Gouache on paper
40 x 30cm (16 x 12in)
Chris Beetles Gallery,
London

This artist revels in the
bright colours and strong
patterns that are found
in both natural and man-
made objects. She finds
that gouache is the perfect
medium to give her the
fluidity and richness suited
to her interpretation.

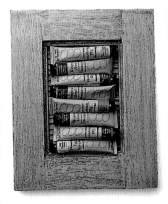

# Egg tempera

Egg-tempera paint has a long and venerable history, and it was universally used by artists until the fifteenth century. Then a method of mixing oils into tempera pigments, in order to give them greater flexibility, eventually produced a pure oil medium which supplanted tempera.

**Basic palette**
**Manufactured-tempera colours are all relatively transparent, and all have a high degree of permanence. The colours cannot be mixed on the support. A starting selection would be similar to that described for gouache, but the technique used for building up tones with small strokes means that the artist develops a personal palette, depending on the subjects chosen.**

## Paints

Tempera is a water-based paint which is made by mixing egg yolk with pigments and distilled water. As this mixture dries on the painting surface, the water evaporates, leaving a hard, thin layer of colour which is extremely durable.

Prepared egg-tempera colours are now available from a few paint manufacturers, although their formulations do vary, so check before buying. Daler-Rowney, for example, produce a range of egg-tempera paints, which are based on a nineteenth-century recipe for an emulsion made from egg yolk and linseed oil. The oil makes the paint slower-drying, more flexible and easier to manipulate, yet it remains water-thinnable. However, because the colour range of ready-made tempera paints is relatively limited, many artists working in tempera still prefer to prepare their own paints, using the vast range of colour pigments that are now available. A basic palette for beginners is shown opposite. Also include titanium white.

**The ASTM (American Society for Testing and Materials) codes for lightfastness:**
**ASTM I: excellent lightfastness**
**ASTM II: very good lightfastness**
**ASTM III: not sufficiently lightfast**

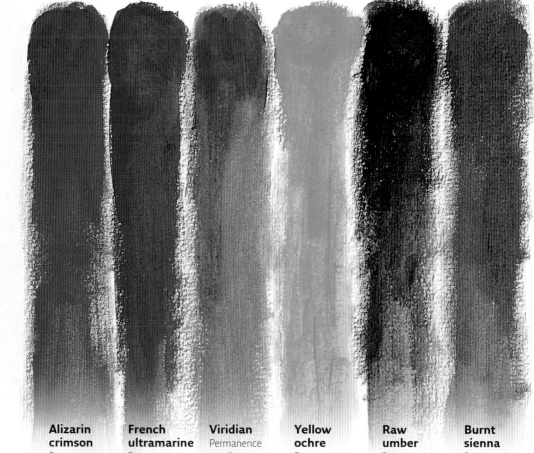

**Cadmium yellow**
Permanence good (ASTM II).

**Alizarin crimson**
Permanence good (ASTM II).

**French ultramarine**
Permanence good (ASTM II).

**Viridian**
Permanence excellent (ASTM I).

**Yellow ochre**
Permanence excellent (ASTM I).

**Raw umber**
Permanence excellent (ASTM I).

**Burnt sienna**
Permanence excellent (ASTM I).

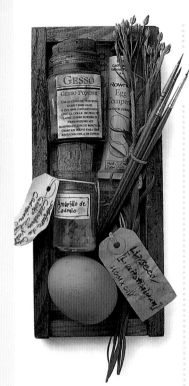

## Techniques

Tempera is not a spontaneous medium, but it is suited to artists who enjoy using a meticulous technique. The paint dries within seconds of application, so colours cannot be blended on the support as they can with other media. Instead, tones and colours are built up with thin colour applied in glazes, or with tiny, hatched strokes. Any number of coats can be superimposed without the finished painting losing any of its freshness. Indeed, repeated layers of translucent colour enhance, rather than diminish, the luminous clarity of tempera.

## Different 'temperas'

Tempera paints are no longer made exclusively with egg, and thus the term tempera has also come to cover emulsions of various sorts. Some paint manufacturers on the European continent, for example, will refer to their gouache paints as 'tempera', so you should always check labels carefully and ask the staff in the art store before buying any tempera paints.

## Surfaces

Tempera can be used on a wide variety of supports, including canvas panels and paper, but the traditional ground is still gesso-primed board, where the smooth, brilliant-white surface reflects light back through the paint, giving the colours their extraordinary luminosity.

## Underpainting for oils

Tempera can also make a wonderful underpainting for oils. When tempera is applied to a white ground, the colour gleams through each layer, giving a painting a distinctive deep, luminous glow.

## Brushes

Round sables or synthetics with a good point are the best brushes to use for tempera painting. The long-haired varieties, such as riggers and lettering brushes, are the most suitable ones

**Pigments**
**Commercial pigments that are suitable for making tempera paints can be purchased from art shops.**

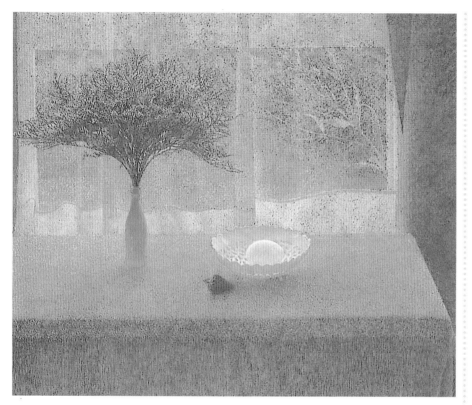

**David Tindle**
*Strawberry*
Egg tempera on board
58.5 x 81.3cm
(23⅜ x 32½in)
Fischer Fine Art, London

As a painter in the quiet, Romantic tradition, David Tindle is concerned with small, intimate, domestic subjects. He uses pure egg tempera and a delicate, painstaking application of tiny hatched marks to portray the disembodying effect of light filtered through a curtained window, thereby reducing solid objects to veils of luminous tone.

because they hold more colour and thus can be worked for longer than short-haired brushes. As tempera dries quite quickly, brushes must be washed frequently in distilled or boiled water.

## Tempera blocks
These are a solid form of gouache which can be used to render colour washes. They are sometimes used for underpainting because they dry rapidly.

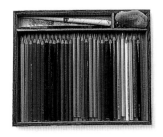

# Water-soluble pencils

These offer all the advantages of normal coloured pencils but they include a water-soluble ingredient in the lead, so that it is possible to thin out their colour into a transparent wash.

## How to use them

You can apply the colour dry, as you would with an ordinary coloured pencil, and you can also use a wet watercolour brush, a wet sponge, or even a wet finger, to loosen the pigment particles and create a subtle watercolour effect. When the washes have dried, you can then add further colour and linear detail, using the pencils dry. If you dampen the paper first, the marks made by the pencil will bleed slightly and produce broad, soft lines. This facility for producing tightly controlled work and loose washes makes water-soluble pencils a flexible medium, and they are very appropriate for rendering natural subjects. They are often used in combination with watercolours, felt-tipped pens, pencil or pen and ink.

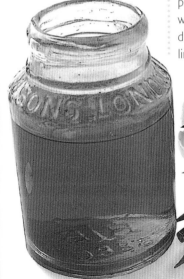

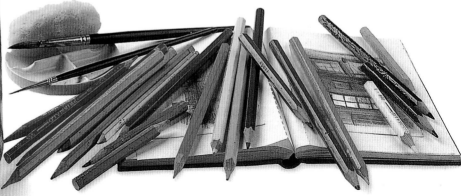

## Techniques

Apply colours with light, hatched strokes, then use a soft brush, rinsed regularly in clean water, to gently blend the strokes and produce a smooth texture. This can take a little practice, as too much water will flood the paint surface and make it blotchy, while insufficient water will prevent the colours blending well; the ideal result resembles a watercolour wash. Heavy pencil strokes will persist and show through the wash.

## Textures

Interesting textures can be created by building up the picture with multiple layers of dry pigment and water-dissolved colour. When adding dry colour over a dissolved base, however, do make sure that the paper is completely dry before you begin. This is because if it is still damp, it will moisten the pencil point and therefore produce a blurred line. In addition, the paper itself may tear.

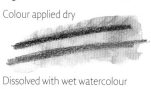

Colour applied dry

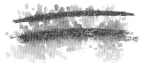

Dissolved with wet watercolour brush

Dissolved with wet sponge

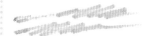

Dissolved with wet finger

Dry point on wet paper

Point dipped in water, on dry paper

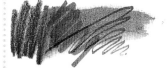

Combined with other materials

**Simon Jennings**
*Greenwich Park*
**Water-soluble pencils, fibre-tip pen and white body colour
Sketchbook page
20.5 x 14.5cm
(8¼ x 5¾in)**

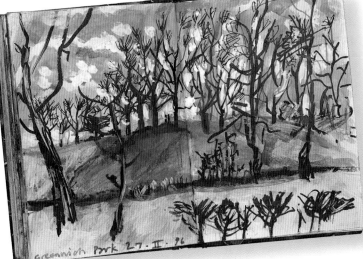

Greenwich Park 27 · II · 96

## Different effects

Water-soluble coloured pencils offer the
artist a surprisingly varied range of effects.
Anna Wood uses water-soluble crayons,
which are thicker and juicier than pencils
and suit her spontaneous way of working.
Suggestions of form, texture and space
emerge from the accidental marks left
as the colour washes spread and dry, as
shown in her study of tomatoes (right).

The astonishing detail and beautiful
texture in David Suff's drawing (opposite)

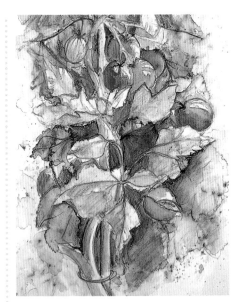

**Anna Wood**
*Tomatoes*
**Water-soluble pencil on paper**
**50 x 35cm (20 x 14in)**

**Albert Jackson**
*Irish Landscape*
**Water-soluble crayons**
**Sketchbook page**
**25 x 17.5cm (10 x 7in)**

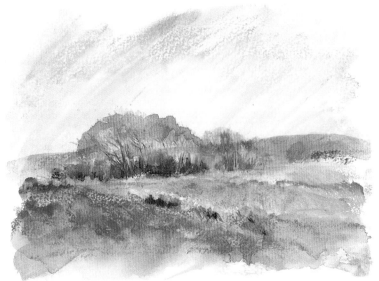

are built up painstakingly with tiny strokes,
which are applied layer upon layer.

Michael Stiff's work (opposite) has a
similar sense of heightened reality. He blends
pastel dust into a smooth layer to produce
basic tonal areas, over which he applies
finely hatched strokes of coloured pencil.

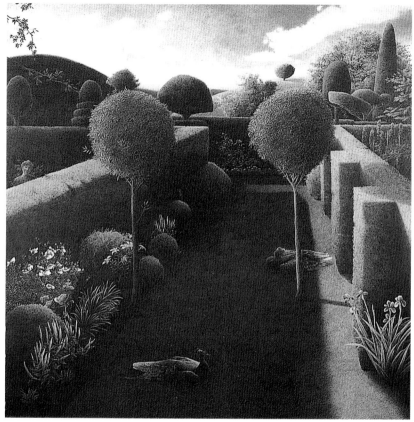

**David Suff**
*The History Garden (Twa Corbies)*
Coloured pencil on paper
90 x 90cm (36 x 36in)

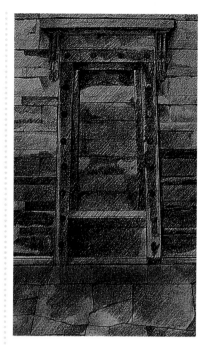

**Michael Stiff**
*Detail, Greek-Thomson Church,*
*Glasgow*
Coloured pencil and pastel on
paper
25 x 20cm (10 x 8in)

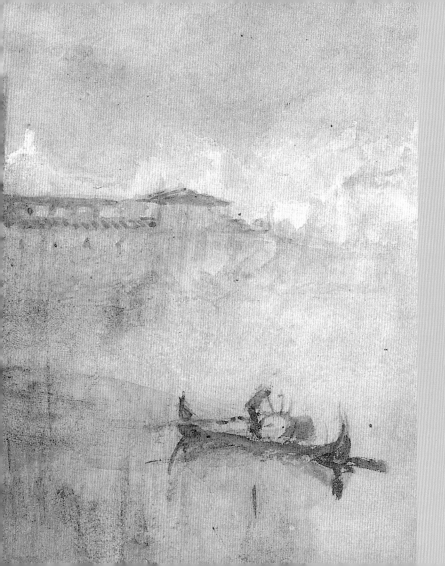

# Watercolour techniques

Watercolour works best when it is expressed as spontaneously and simply as possible. Nevertheless, you still need to learn the basic techniques and try out new ones as you progress. Practise each technique several times and you will soon become more adept and your confidence will grow.

**J.M.W. Turner (1775–1851)**
*Venice Suburb, Moonlight, 1821*
Watercolour on paper
22 x 31.9cm (8¾ x 12¾in)
Tate Gallery, London

# Wash techniques

Washes are the very foundation of watercolour painting. One of the unique qualities of the medium is the way in which light and atmosphere can be conveyed simply by just a few brushstrokes swept over a sheet of sparkling white paper.

**Trees and movement**
Trees can be suggested simply, using nothing more than washes of colour for the foliage. Put in the trunk and branches with loose brushmarks or pen strokes. The bent trees and flying leaves suggest a windy day.

## Choosing paper

The appearance of a wash depends on several factors: the type of pigment used and the level of dilution; the type of paper; and whether the surface is wet or dry when the wash is applied. For example, when washes are applied to an absorbent, low-sized paper, they dry with a soft, diffused quality. On hard-sized paper, wet washes spread more quickly and with less control, but this can create exciting effects. When a wash is laid on dampened paper, the paint goes on very evenly, because the first application of water enables the pigment to spread out on the paper and dissolve without leaving a hard edge. Working on dry paper gives a much sharper, crisper effect, and some painters find it a more controllable method.

## Laying washes

The following tips and guidelines will help you to make successful washes.
• Always mix more colour than you think will be needed to cover an area – you

cannot stop in the middle of laying a wash to mix a fresh supply.

• A watercolour wash dries much lighter than it looks when it is wet, so allow for this when mixing your paint.

• Tilting the board at a slight angle will

allow a wash to flow smoothly downward without dripping.

• Use a large round or flat brush. The fewer and broader the strokes you make, the less risk of any streaks developing.

• Always keep the brush well loaded, but not

Low-sized paper for soft and diffused washes

Medium-sized wet paper for softer washes

Hard-sized paper for quick-spreading washes

Medium-sized dry paper for sharper, crisper washes

**Sized paper**
The effect of painting washes on low-sized paper (far left) and on hard-sized paper (bottom far left).

**Damp or dry paper**
The effect of washes laid on damp paper (left) and dry paper (bottom left), both medium-sized.

Watercolour techniques

83

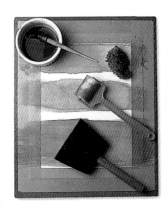

overloaded. Streaking is caused in those instances when a brush is too dry, but if it is overloaded, washes can run out of control.

### Wash-laying equipment
**As well as natural sponges, synthetic-sponge rollers and sponge brushes (left) can be used to lay a smooth wash. For a dense, thick covering, ensure the sponge is filled with plenty of paint. For paler tones or variegated effects, squeeze out some of the paint.**

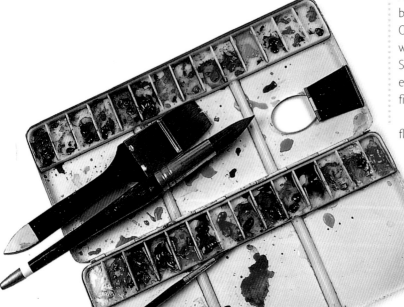

● Don't press too hard. Sweep the brush lightly, quickly and decisively across the paper, using the tip, not the heel.
● Never work back into a previously laid wash to smooth it out – it will only make matters worse.

## Achieving smooth washes
Laying a large, overall wash free of streaks or runs requires a lot of practice. Where heavy washes are to be applied, the paper must be stretched and taped firmly to a board, to prevent cockling or wrinkling. Opinions vary as to whether large areas of wash should be laid on dry or damp paper. Some artists find that a uniform tone is easier to achieve on dry paper, while others find that the paint streaks.

Some watercolourists feel that washes flow more easily on damp paper, whereas others find that slight cockling, even of stretched paper, can produce streaks and marks as the paint collects in the 'dips'. Results vary, too, according to the type of paper that you use; the only answer is to experiment for yourself to see what's best.

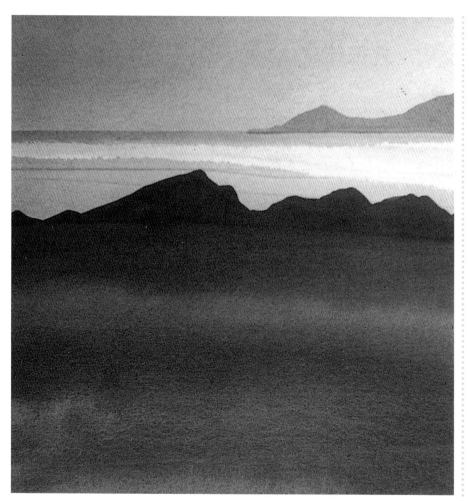

**Robert Tilling**
*Rocks, Low Tide*
Watercolour on paper
50 x 65cm (20 x 26in)

Here Robert Tilling uses the wet-in-wet method to explore the interactions of sky, sea and land. He mixes large quantities of paint in old teacups and applies it with large brushes, tilting his board at an acute angle so that the colours flow down the paper, then reversing the angle to control the flow. When the paper has dried, he paints the dark shapes of rocks and headland wet-on-dry for more crisp definition.

# Flat and graded washes

There are two basic types of wash: a flat wash is evenly toned and is often used to cover the whole area of the paper with a unifying background colour. A graded wash moves gradually from light to dark, dark to light, or one colour to another. It is most often used in painting skies, the colour fading gradually towards the horizon.

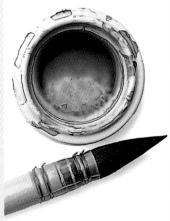

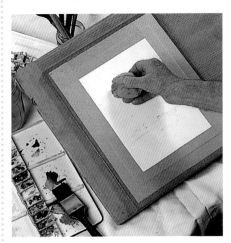

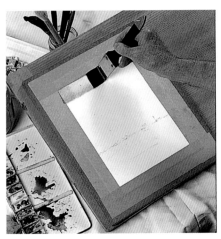

**1 Dampen the paper with a sponge.**
Start by mixing up plenty of colour (in this case, indigo blue) in a saucer or jar. Place the board at a slight angle, and then dampen the paper surface with some water, using either a mop brush or a sponge.

**2 Draw a single stroke across the top.**
Load the brush with paint and draw a single, steady stroke across the top of the area. Due to the angle of the board, a narrow bead of paint will form along the bottom edge of the brushstroke; incorporate this into the next stroke.

## Flat washes

Most watercolourists normally employ flat washes as integral parts of a painting, frequently overlaying one wash with another. However, a flat wash can also be used merely to tint the white paper as a background before the next step of adding the body colour or gouache.

## Laying a basic wash

In the sequence of photographs below, you can see how the artist uses the flat-wash method to create an overall sky effect using diluted indigo blue. Mix up plenty of colour before you start – you don't want to stop and mix more halfway through. Always use clean brushes and sponges.

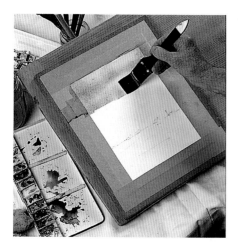

**3 Paint a second stroke below the first.**
Paint a second stroke beneath the first, slightly overlapping it and picking up the bead of paint. Continue down the paper with overlapping strokes, picking up the excess paint from the previous one. Keep the brush well loaded.

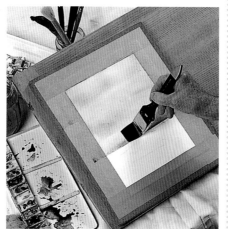

**4 Even up the paint on the base.**
Use a moist, clean brush to even up any paint that gathers along the base of the wash. Leave the painting to dry in the same tilted position, otherwise the paint will flow back and dry, leaving an ugly tidemark.

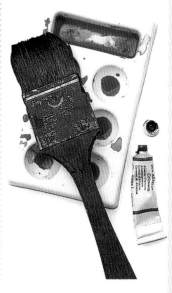

# Graded washes

The method of applying a graded wash is almost exactly the same as for a flat wash (see pages 86–87), except that with each successive brushstroke the brush carries more water and less pigment (or vice versa if you are working from light to dark).

It takes a little practice to achieve a smooth transition in tone, with no sudden jumps. The secret is to apply a sufficient weight of paint so that the excess flows very gently down the surface of the paper, to be merged with the next brushstroke. Allow the colour to spread and even out.

**Wash-laying technique**
In this sequence (right) the graded-wash technique is used to create another sky scene. Cobalt blue is diluted with water in each subsequent brushstroke.

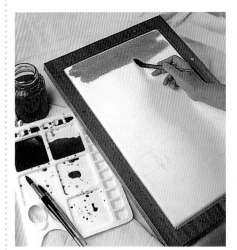

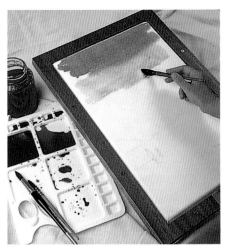

**1 Lay a line of colour at full strength across the top of the paper.**
Dampen the paper as for laying a flat wash (see previous pages), and then lay a line of colour at full strength across the top of the area to be painted. Allow the colour to spread and even out.

**2 Now add some more water and lay a second band of colour.**
Quickly add a little more water to the paint already on your palette and then lay a second band of colour, which should slightly overlap the first. You want to achieve a smooth transition.

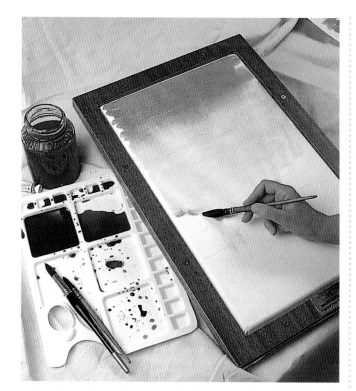

**3 Continue down the paper in the same way, adding more water to the paint with each stroke.**
Continue down the paper, adding more water to the paint with each succeeding stroke and ending with a stroke of pure water. As with flat washes, the brush used to mop up paint along the base of the wash must be clean and moist. Leave to dry in the same tilted position as for flat washes.

## Variegated washes
The technique shown below will enable you to lay two or more colours in a wash.

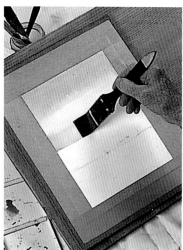

Mix your chosen colours before you start painting, and then apply the first line of colour along the top of the paper. Always washing the brush carefully between colours, apply another colour, partly on blank paper and partly touching the first. Repeat this with any other colours.

## Variety and contrast

A flower painting, a still life and a landscape show some of the variety of techniques and styles that can be achieved with watercolour.

The flower painting (right) belies watercolour's reputation as a medium for old ladies. Blockley attacks his subjects with gusto, using broad household paint brushes to apply vertical streaks of colour.

Watercolour is combined with acrylic paint (right) to give it body while retaining its translucence. Most of the paint is applied wet-in-wet, so the shapes and colours are suggested rather than described.

The evening sky (opposite) has been beautifully described by means of graded washes of pale, pearly colour. The dark tones of the buildings, painted with overlaid washes, accentuate the luminosity of the sky.

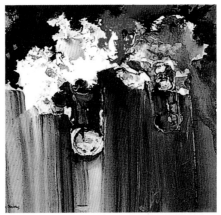

**John Blockley**
*Shop Flowers*
Watercolour on paper
43.2 x 43.2cm
(17 x 17in)

**Sophie Knight**
*Still-life Reflections*
Watercolour and acrylic on paper
35 x 55cm (14 x 22in)

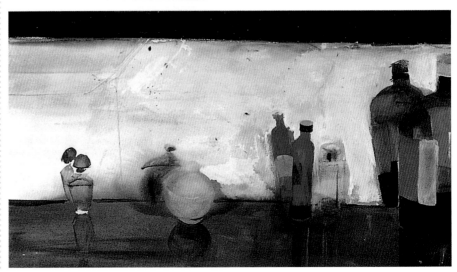

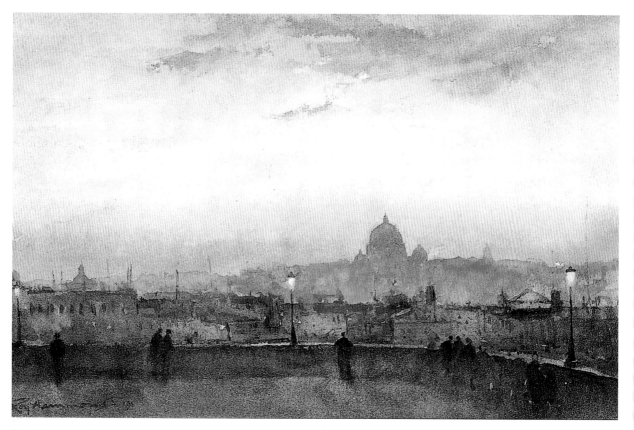

**Roy Hammond**
*London Sunset*
Watercolour on paper
16.2 x 23.7cm (6½ x 9½in)
Chris Beetles Gallery, London

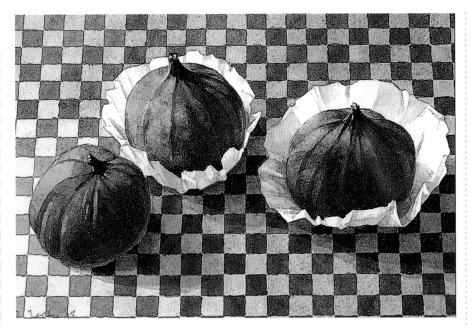

**Ronald Jesty**
*Three Figs*
Watercolour on paper
15 x 20.6cm (6 x 8¼in)

**Penny Anstice (opposite)**
*Nectarines*
Watercolour on paper
30 x 45cm (12 x 18in)

## Different approaches

Experiment with and get to know the characteristics of watercolour. Experience will help you develop a painting style as unique and individual to you as your handwriting style.

It is interesting to compare the different approaches to a similar theme adopted here by Penny Anstice and Ron Jesty. Working on damp paper, Anstice applies wet pools of colour and allows them to flood together, relishing the element of chance that makes wet-in-wet such an exciting technique.

In contrast, Jesty uses a careful and methodical approach, building up form and tone with superimposed washes, which he applies wet-on-dry. He leaves the painting to dry between stages, so the colours aren't muddied but remain crisp and clear.

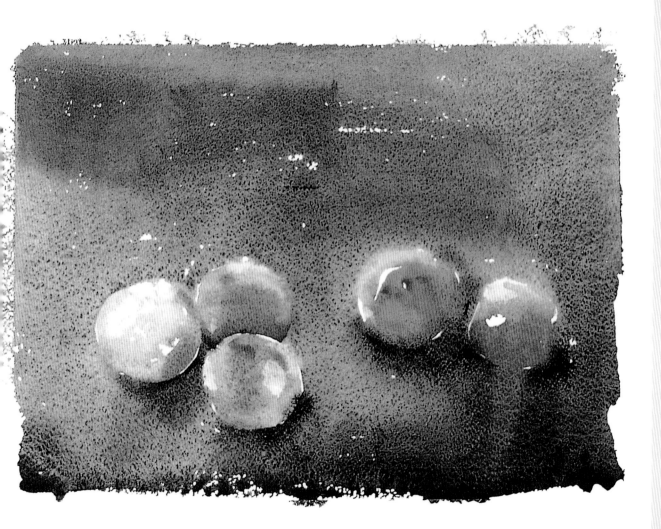

# Wet-in-wet

Wet-in-wet is one of the most expressive and beautiful techniques in watercolour painting. When colours are applied to either a damp sheet of paper or an area of still-wet paint, they run out over the wet surface, giving a soft, hazy edge to the painted shape. This technique is particularly effective in painting skies and water, producing gentle gradations of tone which evoke the ever-changing quality of light.

## Choosing paper

It is essential to choose the right type of paper for wet-in-wet. Avoid papers which are too smooth or which are heavily sized, as the paint tends to sit on the surface. A gently absorbent Not (cold-pressed) surface is ideal, allowing the washes to fuse into the paper structure. The paper should also be robust enough to bear up to frequent applications of water without any cockling. Lighter papers must be stretched and taped to the board. With heavier-grade papers of 410gsm (200lb) or over, you may get away without stretching, but where heavy applications of wash are to be used, it is always best to err on the side of caution.

## Controlling wet-in-wet

Although wet-in-wet painting produces spontaneous effects, it takes practice and experience to be able to judge how wet the paper and the strength of the washes need to be, in order to control the spread and flow of the paint. Use a soft sponge or a large brush to dampen the paper with clean water. The surface should be evenly damp overall; use a tissue to blot up any pools of water, then take your courage in both hands – and your brush in one – and apply the colours.

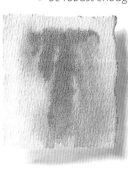

**Wet-in-wet effects**
Paint is applied directly onto wet paper (top). Paint is applied into wet paint (centre). Controlled single-colour paint run on wet paper (right).

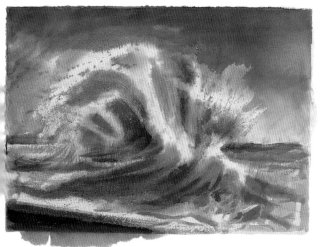

**David Jackson**
*Blue Breaker*
Watercolour on paper
54 x 71cm (21 x 28in)

Fluid, liquid paint is applied generously to dampened paper, wet-in-wet. In places, the white paper shows to represent foam and spray. Colour is lifted out with a sponge and rag, and reapplied to build up the opacity of the sea. Paint is splattered, and the surface scored with a hairbrush – so the paint sinks into the grooves.

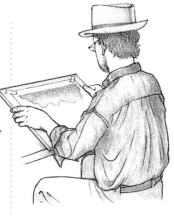

## Applying the paint

Work quickly and confidently, allowing the colours to diffuse and go where they will. Some degree of control can be gained by tilting the board in any direction, but be careful to do this only slightly to allow the colours to flow gently down the paper – this is where the interest and creative tension come in. If a wash does run out of control or goes where you don't want it to be, don't despair; you can lift out some of the colour with a soft, dry brush, or gently blot it with a tissue.

## Dilution and colour

Make sure that you don't over-dilute your paint, as this can make the finished picture appear pale and wan. Because you have wetted the paper, it is possible to use rich paint – but not so thick that it does not spread. The paint will keep its rich hue as it softens on the damp paper. Remember that the colour will appear darker when it is wet and will dry to a lighter shade, particularly where an absorbent paper is used, so do make allowances for this when you are applying paint.

**Tilting the board**
The board should be tilted at an angle of roughly 30 degrees so that the colours can flow gently down the paper. If the board is laid flat, washes cannot spread and diffuse easily, and there will be a danger of colours creeping back into previously laid colours, creating unwanted marks and blotches.

# Wet-on-dry

In this classic technique, tones and colours are applied in a series of pure, transparent layers, one over the other, each wash being allowed to dry thoroughly before the next one is added.

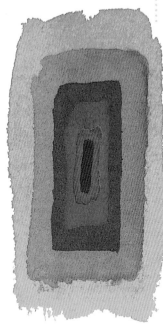

## Superimposed colour

The dry surface of the paper 'holds' the paint, so that brushstrokes will not distort or run out of control. Light travels through each transparent wash to the white paper beneath, and reflects back through the colours. Superimposed washes of thin, pale colour result in more resonant areas of colour than can be achieved by a single, flat wash of dense colour.

### Keeping colours fresh

**If you apply too many layers of paint, the attractive delicacy and freshness of the medium may be lost. Thus it is better to apply a few layers confidently rather than risk muddying the painting by continually adding more. It is always advisable always to test colours by layering them on scrap paper (left) before committing them to the surface. Another common cause of muddy colours is dirty water, so always make sure you rinse your brush thoroughly between colours and take care that you regularly refill your water jar with clean water.**

## Choosing paper

The most suitable paper for the wet-on-dry technique is one which is surface-sized. It should also present a smooth, hard surface which will hold the paint well.

## Be patient

Working wet-on-dry does require a little patience, as each layer must dry before the next one is applied; otherwise the colours will mix and they will become muddied, and the crispness and definition are lost. To speed up the process, you can use a hair dryer on a cool-to-warm setting – let the wash sink in to the paper a little first, otherwise it will get blown around on the paper and will lose its shape.

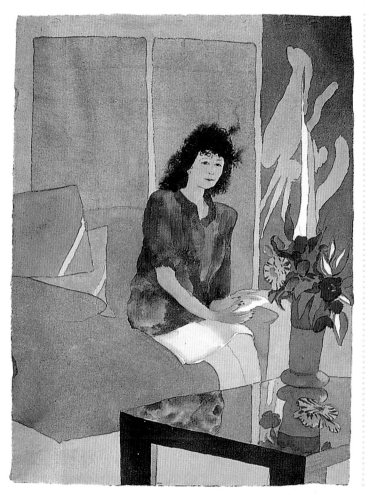

**Patrick Procktor**
*Portrait of Emil Asano*
Watercolour on paper
63.5 x 47cm
(25½ x 18¾in)
Redfern Gallery, London

The success of this painting relies on the simplicity of the design and the controlled, almost restrained, use of two basic watercolour techniques. A series of flat washes indicates the walls and furnishings, capturing the oriental simplicity of the interior. The pattern of the blouse employs the wet-in-wet technique, successfully conveying the softness and fluid colour of the model's costume, which is also reflected in the table top. Note, too, the softness of the hairline against the background, again achieved by working wet-in-wet.

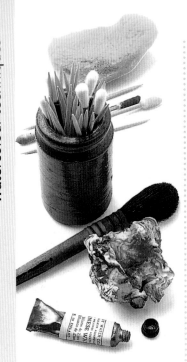

# Creating highlights

Many inexperienced watercolourists make the mistake of trying to cover every part of the paper they are using with paint: in fact, with watercolour this is neither necessary nor desirable.

The light-reflecting surface of watercolour paper provides a uniquely brilliant white which can be used to great effect, adding sparkle to your colours as well as allowing your paintings to 'breathe'. Some of the techniques that are used to manipulate the paint to create white highlights in a watercolour wash are described in the following pages.

**Creating a soft edge**
Use damp paper or blend into the white area with a soft, damp brush.

## Reserving white areas

The simplest way to create white highlights in a watercolour painting is to paint around them, thereby preserving the white of the

**Hercules B. Brabazon
(1821-1906)**
*Cadiz, 1874*
**Watercolour and body colour on tinted paper
26.2 x 35cm (10½ x 14in)
Chris Beetles Gallery, London**

Although he did not receive public recognition until he was 71, Brabazon's bravura technique and boldly conceived compositions placed him among the most progressive artists of his day. This painting (opposite) is typical of his ability to pare down to the essentials of his subject. It is painted with transparent colour on tinted paper, with rich, creamy accents provided by white body colour overlaid with watercolour.

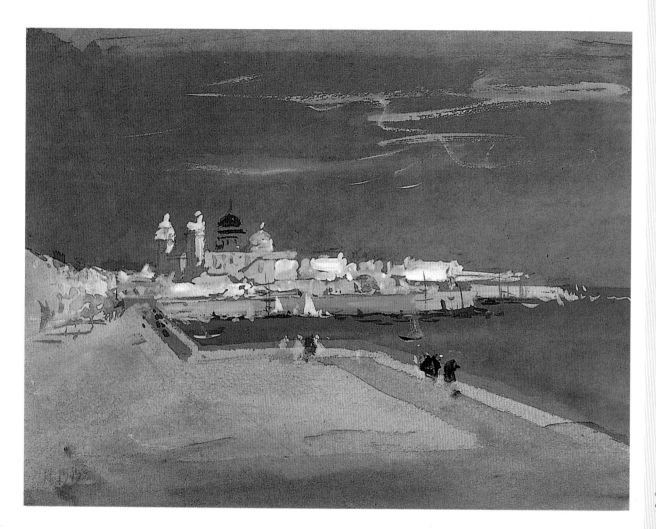

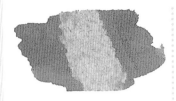

**Lifting out wet paint**
**Use a soft brush, a sponge or tissue for creating soft highlights.**

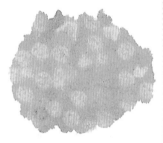

**Lifting out dry paint**
**You can use a damp sponge, a brush or a cotton bud for lifting out.**

paper, with its brilliant light-reflecting properties. Reserving highlights in this way requires careful planning, because it is not always possible to retrieve the pristine white of the paper once a colour has been inadvertently applied.

When you paint around an area to be reserved for a highlight, the paint will dry with a crisp hard edge. For a softer edge, work on damp paper or blend the coloured edges into the white area with a soft, damp brush while the paint is still wet.

## Lifting out

Another method of creating highlights is by gently removing colour from paper while it is still wet, using a soft brush, a sponge or some tissue. This lifting-out technique is often used to create soft diffused highlights, such as the white tops of cumulus clouds. It can also be used to soften edges and

**Using body colour**
**Small amounts of body colour can provide the finishing touches.**

to reveal one colour beneath another. Paint can be lifted out when it is dry by gentle coaxing with a damp sponge, brush or a cotton bud. The results will vary according to the colour to be lifted (for example, strong stainers such as alizarin crimson and phthalocyanine green may leave a faint residue) and the type of paper used (paint is more difficult to remove from soft-sized papers). In some cases, pigment may be loosened more easily using hot water, which partially dissolves the gelatine size used on the surface of the paper.

## Using body colour

Some of the greatest watercolourists, from Dürer to Turner to Sargent, used touches of

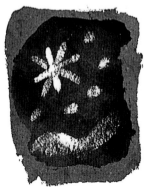

body colour for creating the highlights in their paintings, with some breathtaking results. As long as the opaque parts of your painting are as sensitively and thoughtfully handled as the transparent areas, they will integrate naturally into the whole scheme.

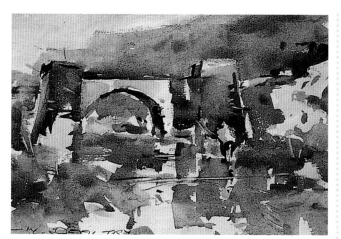

## William Dealtry
*North Yorkshire Stream*
Watercolour on paper
16.2 x 22.5cm (6½ x 9in)
Brian Sinfield Gallery, Burford

In this fresh painting, broad washes
have been rapidly manipulated with
a flat brush, simplifying the scene
almost to abstraction, yet keeping its
essential character. The unpainted
areas serve to give an impression of
movement and changing light.

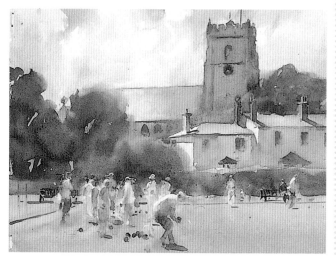

## Trevor Chamberlain
*Bowls Match, Sidmouth*
Watercolour on paper
22.5 x 30cm (9 x 12in)

Trevor Chamberlain's painting of a
quintessential country scene exudes
an air of calm and tranquillity. The
effect of sunlight glancing off the
players' white shirts is skillfully wrought
by means of judicious lifting out of
colour to create suffused highlights.

# Masking out

Because of the transparent nature of watercolours, light colours and tones cannot be painted over dark ones, as they can in oils or acrylics. Light or white areas must be planned initially and painted around. This is not difficult for broad areas and simple shapes, but preserving small shapes, such as highlights on water, can be a nuisance, as the method inhibits the flow of the wash. One solution is to seal off these areas first with some masking fluid, thus freeing yourself from the worry of painting accidentally over the areas that you wish to keep white.

## Using masking fluid

Masking fluid is a liquid, rubbery solution which is applied to paper with a brush. It dries very quickly to form a water-resistant film

**Masking fluid**
**This is a rubbery solution that prevents colour soaking into the paper. It is used primarily to mask off fine details and highlights that would be difficult to paint in later with opaque body colour.**

which protects the paper underneath it. When both the masking fluid and surrounding paint are dry, the fluid can be removed very easily by rubbing it either with an eraser or with a clean fingertip.

Masking fluid can also be useful in the later stages of a painting, in order to preserve areas of any specific tone or colour in a surrounding wash. However, always make sure that the area to be preserved is completely dry before applying the fluid.

Ideally, any masking fluid should be removed from a painting within 24 hours of application, otherwise it will be difficult to rub off and may leave a slight residue.

**Blades, abrasive papers and sharpened brush handles make useful highlighting tools.**

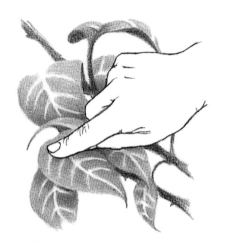

**Erasing masking fluid**
**Use a pencil eraser or a fingertip.**

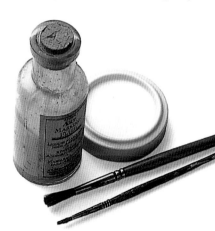

If you intend to use masking fluid, then choose a paper with a Not (cold-pressed) surface, from which it is easily removed; it is not suitable for rough papers, as it sinks into indents and cannot be peeled off completely.

Shake the bottle before using; too-thin fluid will not resist paint. Once opened, a bottle has a shelf life of around one year. Excessive heat can make it unworkable. In hot climates, store it somewhere cool, and work in the shade when applying it to paper.

## Cleaning brushes

Masking fluid is tough on brushes – even with careful cleaning, dried fluid can build up on brush hairs over a period of time. Always use cheap synthetic brushes to apply fluid – not your best sable! The best method of cleaning synthetic brushes is to rinse them in lighter fuel and leave them to dry.

**Masking-fluid effects**
**Masking fluid is invaluable to watercolour painting. You can use it where you want any light areas or highlights to appear in your picture. Apply the paint over the masking fluid and then remove it (above left) to reveal the white of the paper or to show the previously laid colour (right).**

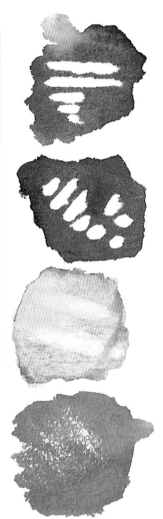

103

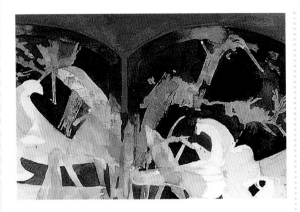

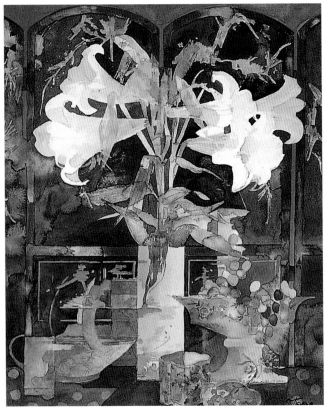

**Shirley Trevena**
*White Lilies on a Patterned Screen*
Watercolour and gouache on paper
45.5 x 35cm (18$\frac{1}{4}$ x 14$\frac{1}{4}$in)

On the oriental screen (see detail above), the patterns were painted with masking fluid before the dark washes were applied. The mask was then removed and the mother-of-pearl colours were painted in.

## Scratching out

You can create fine linear highlights, such as light catching the blades of grass, by scratching out of a painted surface when it is dry. To do this, use a sharp, pointed tool, for instance a scalpel or craft knife, or even a razor blade. Work gently by degrees to avoid digging the blade into the paper and tearing the surface.

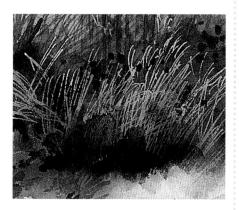

## Diffused highlights

A diffused highlight, such as the pattern of frothy water on ocean waves or waterfalls, can be made by scraping the surface gently with the side of the blade of a scalpel or craft knife, or even with a piece of fine

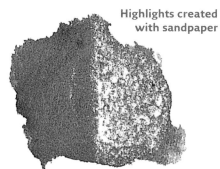

**Highlights created with sandpaper**

sandpaper. This removes the colour from the raised tooth of the paper only, leaving colour in the indents and creating a mottled, broken-colour effect.

More delicate, muted highlights can be scratched out of paint that is not quite dry, using the tip of a paintbrush handle or your fingernail – Turner is said to have grown one fingernail long, especially for scratching out highlights from his watercolours.

**Scratched highlights and marks**
**The examples here show four ways of creating highlights: (from top to bottom) scratching with a blade point; scratching with a blade edge; scraping with a blunt paintbrush handle; and scraping with a sharpened brush handle.**

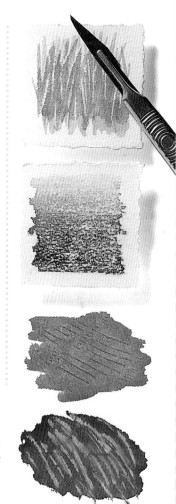

# Textures and effects

One of the main attractions of watercolour is its freshness and immediacy – its power to suggest without overstatement. There are many techniques you can use to create the desired effects.

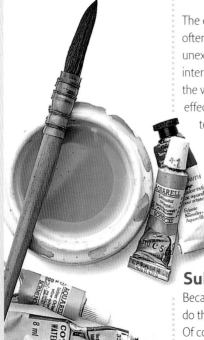

The experienced artist knows that, very often, magical things can happen quite unexpectedly when water and pigment interact on paper; the paint actually does the work for you, producing atmospheric effects or patterns that resemble natural textures. A 'bloom' appears in a wash, resembling a storm cloud; a wash dries with a slightly grainy quality that adds interest to a foreground; or a swiftly executed brushstroke catches on the ridges of the paper, leaving a broken, speckled mark suggestive of light on water.

## Subtlety and restraint

Because these effects occur naturally, they do the job without appearing laboured. Of course, it is also possible for the artist to adopt an interventionist approach and deliberately manipulate the paint or even

add things to it, in order to imitate certain textures and surface effects. Some of these techniques are described below, but it is very important to realize that, if they are overdone, texturing techniques can easily appear facile. You should only ever use them with subtlety and restraint, so that they are incorporated naturally within the painting as a whole.

**Granulation of pigments**
**Certain watercolour pigments separate out, giving a granular effect which can be subtly descriptive and expressive. In each of the paintings opposite, the artists have made quite deliberate use of granulation. It enlivens the background wash in Patrick Procktor's portrait, while Robert Tilling has used it to suggest subtle, atmospheric effects in the evening sky and landscape.**

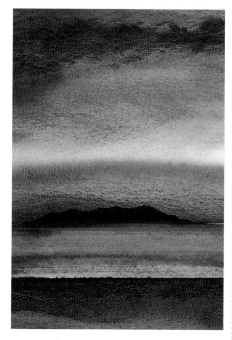

**Robert Tilling (above)**
*Evening Light*
Watercolour on paper
65 x 50cm (26 x 20in)

**Patrick Procktor (right)**
*Vasco*
Watercolour on paper
50.8 x 35.5cm (20⅜ x 14¼in)
Redfern Gallery, London

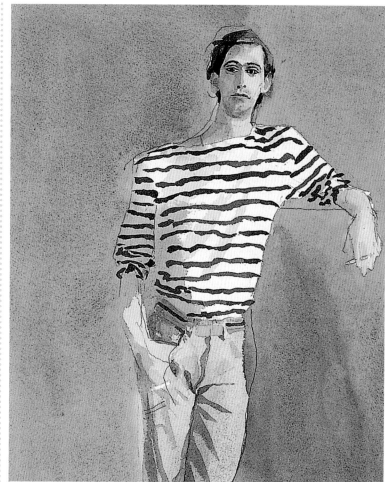

*'In my case, all painting is an accident... it transforms itself by the actual paint. I don't, in fact, know very often what the paint will do, and it does many things which are very much better than I could make it do. Perhaps one could say it's not an accident, because it becomes part of the process which part of the accident one chooses to preserve.'*
**Francis Bacon (1909-92)**

# Granulation

This is a phenomenon which often occurs seemingly by accident, yet it can impart a beautiful, subtle texture to a wash. Certain watercolour pigments show a tendency to precipitate: the pigment particles of the earth colours, for example, are fairly coarse. As the wash dries, tiny granules of pigment float in the water and settle in the hollows of paper, producing a mottled effect.

Only experience and experimentation will enable you to tell just how much granulation may take place. For example, some colours granulate only when they are laid over a previous wash. In other cases, granulation may not happen at all, or may be hardly noticeable, if the paint is heavily diluted. As you become more proficient as a painter, you will know in advance.

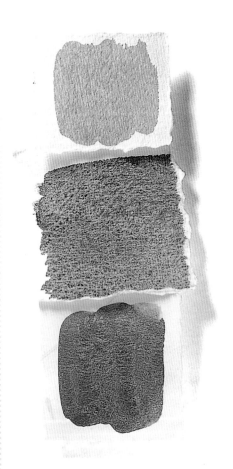

**Pigment granulation**
Some pigments show a tendency to granulate or flocculate, producing subtly textured washes, while others produce flat and even washes. An understanding of how the different pigments behave will open up many exciting possibilities for creating particular effects.

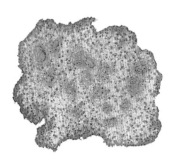

Experiment with various colours and makes to find out which pigments tend to granulate or flocculate.

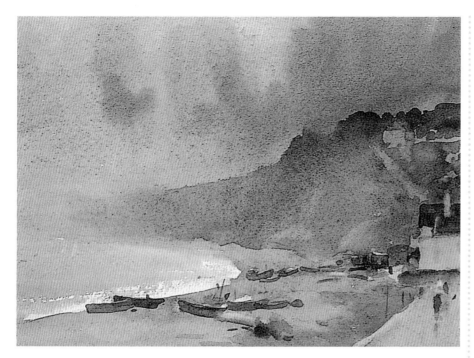

**Trevor Chamberlain**
*Rain at Budleigh Salterton*
**Watercolour on paper
17.5 x 25cm (7 x 10in)**

**In this painting the artist
has made deliberate use
of granulation to suggest
subtle, atmospheric effects
in the sky and landscape.**

## Flocculation

A similar grainy effect can be produced by pigments, such as French ultramarine, which flocculate – the pigment particles are attracted to each other rather than dispersing evenly. This will cause a slight speckling which, in turn, can lend a wonderful atmospheric quality to your paintings, especially skies and landscapes.

Simply by experimenting with different watercolour paints, and by knowing which colours have this settling tendency, it is possible for you to suggest all sorts of different textures in your paintings, such as weatherbeaten rocks, newly fallen snow, or sand, quite effortlessly.

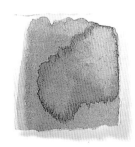

# Blooms

Blooms, or backruns, will sometimes occur when a wet wash is flooded into another, drier wash; as the second wash spreads, it dislodges some of the pigment particles beneath. These particles collect at the edge of the wash as it dries, thereby creating a pale, flower-like shape with a dark, crinkled edge.

## By accident or design?

Although most blooms are usually accidental, and often unwanted, they can be used to create some textures and effects that are difficult to obtain using normal painting methods. For example, a series of small blooms creates a mottled pattern suggestive of weathered, lichen-covered stone; in landscapes, blooms can represent amorphous shapes, such as distant hills, trees and clouds, or ripples on the surface of a stream, and they can add texture and definition to the forms of leaves and flowers.

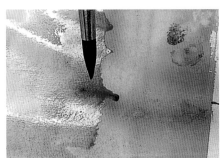

**Making small blooms**
Small, circular blooms are formed by dropping paint from the end of a brush into a damp wash. You can also create pale blooms in a darker wash by just dropping clear water into it.

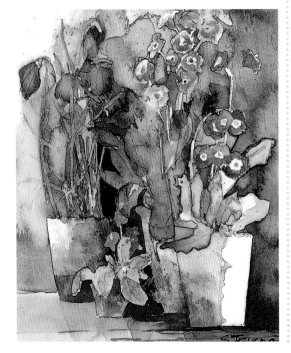

**Shirley Trevena**
*Four Flowerpots*
Watercolour on paper
27.5 x 21.5cm
(11 x 8⅝in)

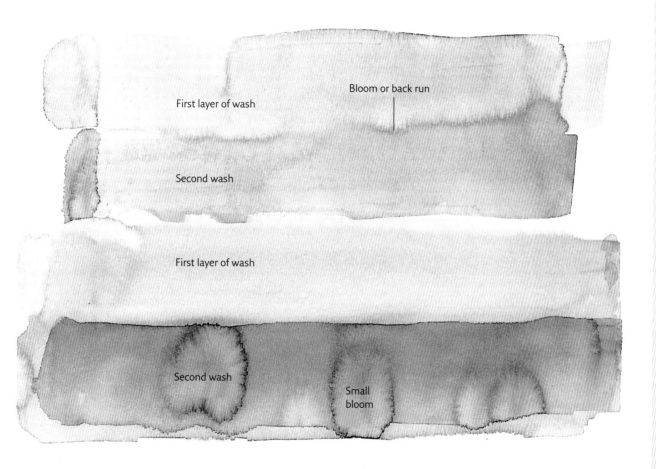

First layer of wash

Bloom or back run

Second wash

First layer of wash

Second wash

Small bloom

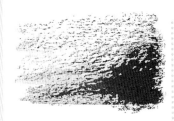

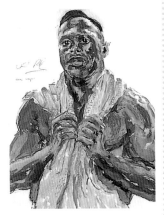

**Hans Schwarz**
*Glazz Campbell, after
Training*
**Watercolour on paper
80 x 55cm (32 x 22in)**

**John Lidzey**
*Cottage Bedroom*
**Watercolour on paper
30 x 30cm (12 x 12in)**

# Drybrush

The drybrush technique is invaluable in watercolour painting, because it can suggest complex textures and details by an economy of means. It is used most often in landscape painting, to suggest a range of natural effects such as sunlight on water, the texture of rocks and tree bark, or the movement of clouds and trees.

Moisten your brush with a very little water, and then take up a small amount of paint on the tip. Remove any excess moisture by flicking the brush across a paper tissue or a dry rag before lightly and quickly skimming the brush over dry paper.

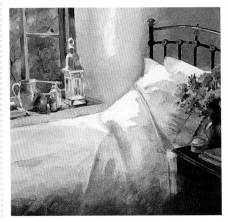

# Unpredictable effects

The experienced watercolourist will have experimented with a range of techniques, and knows how to exploit the element of 'happy accident' in the paint.

The mercurial, unpredictable nature of watercolour is one of its chief joys. In the still-life paintings on this page, both artists have used the descriptive potential of backruns to suggest textures and enrich the picture surface.

# Brushmarks and effects

Brushmarks and effects play a vital and expressive part in watercolour painting. Hans Schwarz (far left) has used a bold and direct approach, the brushmarks following and sculpting the forms of the face and figure to create a lively, energetic portrait.

John Blockley's painting method (opposite right) involves a continual and daring process. He makes some areas wetter than others, then dries only some parts with a hair dryer. He then plunges the painting into a bath of water; the dry paint remains intact, but the wet paint floats off, leaving some areas of white paper lightly stained with colour.

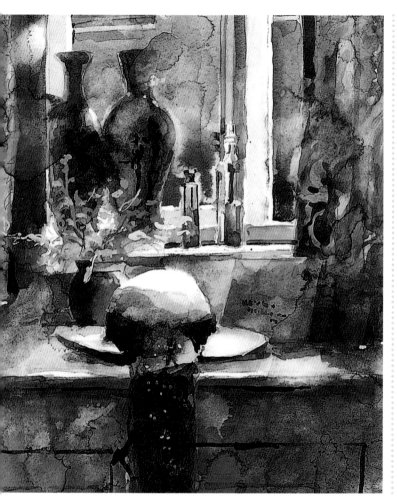

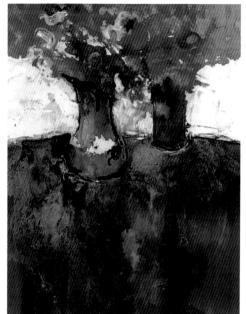

**John Blockley**
*Table Flowers*
Watercolour on paper
47 x 38cm (18½ x 15in)


**John Lidzey**
*Interior with Hat*
Watercolour on paper
45 x 30cm (18 x 12in)

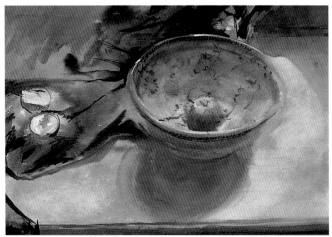

**Sophie Knight**
*China Bowl with Fruit*
**Watercolour on paper**
**55 x 75cm (22 x 30in)**

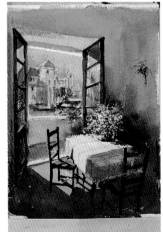

**Gerald Green**
*Interior*
**Watercolour on paper**
**35 x 25cm (13½ x 10in)**

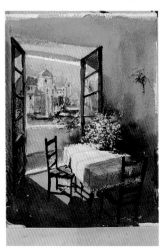

**John Lidzey**
*A Woman Dressing at the Dell*
**Watercolour on paper**
**50.5 x 35.5cm (20 x 14in)**

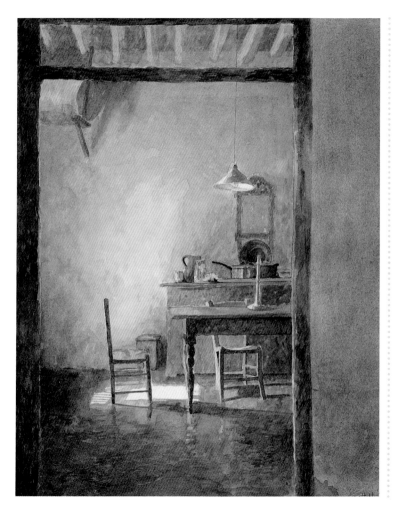

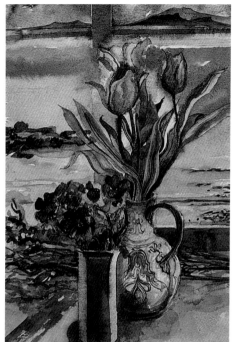

**John Mitchell (above)**
*Studio Window*
Watercolour on paper
33 x 25cm (13 x 10in)

**Annie Williams (left)**
*The Kitchen*
Watercolour on paper
58.5 x 45.5cm (23 x 16in)

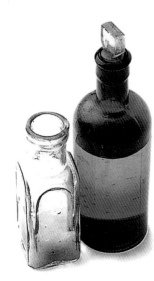

**Turpentine, salt and wax can be used to create unpredictable textures.**

## Using salt

Unpredictable effects can be obtained by scattering grains of coarse rock salt into wet paint. The salt crystals soak up the paint around them; when the picture is dry and the salt is brushed off, a pattern of pale, crystalline shapes is revealed. These delicate shapes are extremely effective in creating the illusion of falling snow in a winter landscape, or for adding a hint of texture to stone walls and rock forms.

Although initially this may seem an easy technique, timing the application of salt does require some practice. The wash should ideally be somewhere between wet and damp – neither too wet nor too dry. Applying salt to a wet wash will create large, soft shapes, whereas applying it to a barely damp wash will produce smaller, more

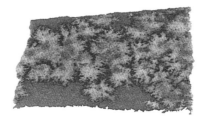

**Using salt**
As salt crystals soak up paint, a pattern of shapes will emerge.

granulated shapes. Apply the salt sparingly to a horizontal surface, let it dry thoroughly, and then brush the salt off.

## Using a sponge

Painting with a sponge creates textures and effects which may be impossible to render with a brush. For example, a mottled pattern suggesting clumps of foliage or the surface of weathered stone may be produced just by dabbing with a sponge dipped in some paint. Always use a natural sponge, which is softer and more absorbent than a synthetic sponge, and which has an irregular, more interesting texture.

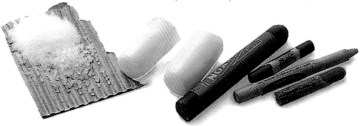

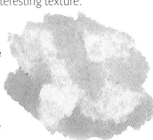

**Using a sponge**
Apply paint lightly with a natural sponge to create some textural effects.

# Wax resist

A broken texture can be created by rubbing or drawing with a white wax candle or a coloured wax crayon and then overpainting with watercolour. Wax adheres unevenly to paper, catching on the raised tooth and leaving the hollows untouched. When a colour wash is applied, the wax repels the paint, causing it to coagulate in droplets. The broken, batik-like effect created by wax resist can be used to suggest textures and surface effects, such as rocks, tree bark, sand, or light on water or grass.

This technique works best on a Not or rough surface. Skim a candle or wax crayon across the paper so that it touches the high points but not the indents, then apply your watercolours in the normal way. When the painting is completely dry, the wax can be removed by covering it with absorbent paper and pressing with a cool iron until the paper has absorbed all the melted wax.

## Using turpentine

In a variation on the resist technique, turpentine or white spirit can be sparingly applied to well-sized paper, allowed to dry slightly and then painted over. The paint and the oil will separate, thereby creating an interesting marbled effect.

**Using a candle**
**You can paint over rubbed- or drawn-on wax to create natural-looking textures.**

**Using turpentine**
**Another version of the resist method involves applying turpentine.**

117

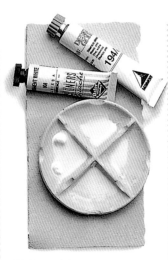

# Gouache techniques

Gouache is still somewhat underrated as a painting medium, considering how versatile it is. Like watercolour, it can be thinned with water to a fluid consistency, but its relative opacity gives it a more rugged quality, which is ideal for bold, energetic paintings and rapid landscape sketches.

When it is wet, gouache can be scrubbed, scratched and scumbled, and interesting things happen as colours run together and form intricate marbled and curdled patterns.

## Washes and tones

Gouache is equally suitable for creating a more delicate, lyrical style of painting, in which washes of thin, semi-transparent colour are built up in layers which dry with a soft, matt, velvety appearance.

With gouache colours, tones may be lightened either by adding white or by thinning the paint with water, depending on the effect you wish to achieve. Thinning with water gives gouache a semi-opaque, milky quality, whereas adding white gives a dense, opaque covering.

**Using white**
There are two whites available: permanent white (sometimes called titanium white) and zinc white. Permanent white has the greater covering power; zinc white is cool and subtle.

**Lightening tones**
These examples (right) demonstrate how gouache colours can be modified by adding either water or white paint.

Added white paint

Thinned with water

## Painting dark-over-light

Gouache is technically an opaque paint, so you can, in theory, apply light colours over dark. In practice, however, it is best to stick to the dark-over-light method, as gouache is not as opaque as oils or acrylics – in fact, some colours are only semi-opaque. Gouache will completely cover a colour if it is used very thick and dry, but this is not advisable, as it may lead to subsequent cracking of the paint surface.

## Solubility

Because gouache colours contain relatively little binder, they remain soluble when dry, so an application of wet colour may pick up some colour from the layer below. This can be prevented by allowing one layer to dry completely before applying the next. Apply the paint with a light touch, and avoid overbrushing your colours.

Scrubbed and scumbled

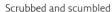

Scratched

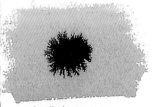

Curdled patterns

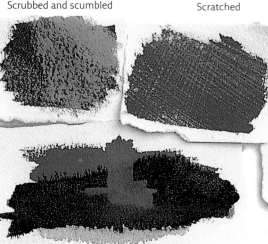

Light paint over dark

**Versatile gouache**
These sketchbook examples illustrate the versatility of gouache paint and show the relative opacity of this underrated medium.

**Making and using gouache impasto**
The impasto technique is usually associated with oil or acrylic painting, but the addition of impasto gel turns gouache or watercolour paint into a thick, malleable paste. You should mix the gel approximately half-and-half with the paint, and apply to the support with a knife or a brush to make textured effects.

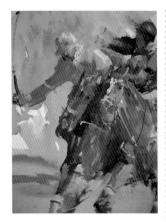

**Jane Camp**
*Last Chukka*
Gouache on paper
35 x 25cm (14 x 10in)
Westcott Gallery, Dorking

This is a marvellous
example of the fluid and
vigorous use of gouache
to convey movement and
energy. The beauty of the
medium is its ability to
create appropriate textural
marks, almost of its own
free will.

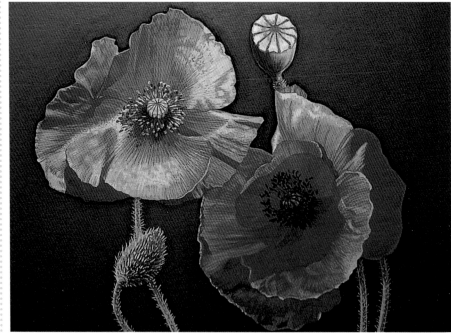

**Sally Keir**
*Red Poppies*
Gouache on paper
24 x 26.5cm (9⅜ x 10⅜in)

Although lacking the luminous effect of pure watercolour,
gouache has a light-reflecting quality that is ideally
suited to flower studies. This painting has the clarity and
detail of botanical illustration, but the vibrant intensity of
gouache colours keeps the subject alive.

# Glossary of terms

**ASTM** American Society for Testing and Materials. An internationally recognized, independent standard for certain paint qualities, used by most manufacturers.

**Balance** In a work of art, the overall distribution of forms and colour to produce a harmonious whole.

**Blending** Smoothing the edges of two colours together so that they have a smooth gradation where they meet.

**Body colour** Opaque paint, such as gouache, which has the covering power to obliterate underlying colour.

**Brushwork** The characteristic way in which each artist brushes paint onto a support; also used to help attribute paintings to a particular artist.

**Casein** A milk-protein-based binder mixed with pigment to make paint; most often associated with tempera.

**Cockling** Wrinkling or puckering in paper supports, caused by applying washes onto flimsy or inadequately stretched and prepared surface.

**Composition** The arrangement of elements in a painting or drawing.

**Contre-jour** (French for 'against the daylight') A painting or drawing where the light source is behind the subject.

**Earth colours** The umbers, siennas and ochres, which are regarded as the most stable natural pigments.

**Film** A thin coating or layer of paint, etc.

**Fixative** A solution, usually of shellac and alcohol, sprayed onto drawings, particularly charcoal, chalk and soft pastels, to prevent them smudging or crumbling off the support.

**Format** Proportions and size of support.

**Fugitive colours** Pigment or dye colours that fade when exposed to light. (See also lightfast and permanence.)

**Genre** A category or type of painting, classified by its subject matter – still life, landscape, portrait, etc. The term is also applied to scenes depicting domestic life.

**Gesso** A mixture, usually composed of whiting and glue size, used as a primer for rigid oil-painting supports.

**Glaze** A transparent or semi-transparent colour laid over another, different colour to modify or intensify it.

**Grain** *See* tooth.

**Ground** A specially prepared painting surface.

**Gum arabic** A gum, extracted from certain Acacia trees, used in solution as a medium for watercolour paints.

**Hatching** A technique of modelling, indicating tone and suggesting light and shade in drawing or tempera painting, using closely set parallel lines.

**Hue** The name of a colour – blue, red, yellow, etc. – irrespective of its tone or intensity.

**Imprimatura** A primary coat of diluted colour, usually a wash, used to tone down or tint a white canvas or other support before painting.

121

**Intensity** Purity and brightness of a colour. Also called saturation or chroma.

**Key** Used to describe the prevailing tone of a painting: a predominantly light painting is said to have a high key, a predominantly dark one a low key.

**Leaching** The process of drawing out excess liquid through a porous substance.

**Lightfast** Term applied to pigments that resist fading when exposed to sunlight. (*See also* fugitive.)

**Local colour** The actual colour of an object or surface, unaffected by shadow colouring, light quality or other factors; for instance, the local colour of a carrot is always orange, even with a violet shadow falling across it.

**Medium** This term has two distinct meanings which are as follows: the first is the liquid in which pigments are suspended, for instance, linseed oil for oil painting, and acrylic resin for acrylic paints (the plural here is mediums). However, a medium is also the material chosen by the artist for working – paint, ink, pencil, pastel, etc. (the plural in this instance is media).

**Mixed media** In drawing and painting, this refers to the use of different media in the same picture – for instance, ink, watercolour wash and wax crayon – or on a combination of supports – for instance, newspaper and cardboard.

**Opacity** The covering or hiding ability of a pigment to obliterate an underlying colour. Opacity varies between pigments.

**Palette** As well as describing the various forms of holders and surfaces for mixing paint colours, palette also refers to the artist's choice and blends of colours when painting.

**Permanence** This refers to a pigment's resistance to fading on exposure to sunlight. Art materials manufacturers supply details as to the permanence of individual colours in their product ranges. (*See also* fugitive and lightfast.)

**Pigments** The colouring agents that are used in all painting and drawing media, traditionally manufactured from natural plant and mineral sources but now including synthetic man-made substances. The word is also used to describe the powdered or dry forms of the agents.

**Plasticity** In a two-dimensional drawing or painting, plasticity describes figures, objects or space with a strongly three-dimensional appearance, often achieved by modelling with great contrasts of tone,

**Plein air** (French for 'open air') A term describing paintings that are done outside on location, directly from the subject.

**Primary colours** The three primary colours – red, yellow and blue – are so called because they cannot be mixed from other colours.

**Proportion** The relationship of one part to the whole or to other parts. This can refer to, for instance, the relation of each component of the human figure to the figure itself, or to the painting as a whole.

**Recession** In art, this describes the effect of making objects appear to recede into the distance by the use of aerial perspective and colour.

**Reduction** The result of mixing colour with white.

**Sanguine** A red-brown chalk.

**Saturation** The intensity and brilliance of a colour.

**Scumble** The technique of dragging one or more layers of dryish, opaque paint over a bottom layer that partially shows through the overlying ones.

**Sgraffito** (Italian for 'scratched off') A technique of scoring into a layer of colour with a sharp instrument, to reveal either the ground colour or a layer of colour beneath.

**Shade** The term for a colour darkened with black.

**Shaped canvas** Any non-rectangular picture.

**Size** A weak glue solution which is used for making gesso and distemper, for stiffening paper.

**Size colour** A combination of hot glue size and pigments.

**Sketch** A rough drawing or a preliminary draft of a composition, which is not necessarily to be worked up subsequently. Sketches are often used as a means of improving an artist's observation and technique.

**Staining colours** A term that refers particularly to watercolours. Some colours are made from very finely ground particles of pigment and they may not be completely 'lifted out' from the paper if required.

**Study** A detailed drawing or painting made of one or more parts of a final composition, but not of the whole.

**Support** A surface which is used for painting or drawing: canvas, board, paper, etc.

**Tempering** In painting, mixing pigments with tempera to produce a hue.

**Tint** Term for a colour lightened with white. Also, in a mixture of colours, the tint is the dominant colour.

**Tinting strength** The power of a pigment to influence mixtures of colours.

**Tone** The relative darkness or lightness of a colour, without reference to its local colour.

**Tooth** The texture, ranging from coarse to fine, of canvas or wood.

**Tragacanth** A gum, which is extracted from certain Astragalus plants, and then used as a binding agent in watercolour paints and pastels.

**Transparency** The state of allowing light to pass through, and of filtering light.

**Value** An alternative word for 'tone', 'value' is used mainly in the United States. The term 'tonal value' refers to the relative degree of lightness or darkness of any colour, on a scale of greys running from black to white.

**Vehicle** A medium that carries pigments in suspension and makes it possible to apply them to a surface; sometimes called the base. Also describes a combination of medium and binder.

**Volume** The space that a two-dimensional object or figure fills in a painting.

**Wash** A thin, usually broadly applied, layer of transparent or heavily diluted paint or ink.

**Wetting agent** A liquid – oxgall or a synthetic equivalent – added to watercolour paint to help it take evenly and smoothly on a support.

# Suppliers and sources

### Berol (watersoluble pencils)

**Berol Ltd**
Berol House
Oldmedow Road
King's Lyn
Norfolk PE30 4JR
www.berol.co.uk

### Canson (watercolour papers)

**ArjoWiggins Fine Papers Pty Ltd**
Fine Papers House
PO Box 88,
Lime Tree Way
Chineham
Basingstoke
Hants RG24 8BA
Tel: 01256 728728
www.arjowiggins.com

### Caran d'Ache
(watersoluble pencils)

**Jakar International Ltd**
Hillside House
2–6 Friern Park,
London N12 9BX
Tel: 0208 445 6376
www.jakar.co.uk

### Daler-Rowney
(gouache & watercolour paints; brushes)

**Daler-Rowney Ltd**
PO Box 10
Bracknell
Berkshire
RG12 8ST
Tel: 01344 461000
www.daler-rowney.co.uk

### Faber-Castell
(watersoluble pencils)

**West Design Products Ltd**
Unit 1A
Part Farm Road
Folkestone
Kent CT19 5EH
Tel: 01303 247110
www.faber-castell.com

### Falkiner Fine Papers (paper)

**Falkiner Fine Papers Ltd**
76 Southampton Row
London WC1B 7AR
Tel: 0207 831 1151
Fax: 0207 430 1248
www.falkiners.com

### Gerand (brushes)

**Gerand Brushes**
Gerand House
41 Alric Avenue
London NW10 8RA
Tel: 0207 515 9355
www.gerandart.co.uk

### Inscribe (watercolour paints and brushes; watersoluble pencils)

**Inscribe Ltd**
51 Woolmer Way
Woolmer Industrial Estate
Bordon
Hampshire GU35 9QE
Tel: 01420 475747

### Lefranc & Bourgeois
(watercolour paints and watersoluble pencils)

**Lefranc & Bourgeois**
5 Rue René Panhard
21 Nord 72021 Le Mans
Cedex 2
France
Tel: 02 43 83 83 00
www.lefranc-bourgeois.com

## Pebeo (gouache paints and brushes; watercolour paper)

**Pebeo SA**
Parc D'Activites de Gemenos 305
Avenue du Pic-de-Bertagne
Cedex F-13881
Gemenos
France
Tel: 33 (4) 42 32 08 08
Email: info@pebeo.com
www.pebeo.com

## Pentel (watercolour paint)

**Pentel (Stationery) Ltd**
Hunts Rise
South Marston Park
Swindon
Wiltshire SN3 4TW
Tel: 01793 823333
www.pentel.com

## Pro Arte (brushes)

**Pro Arte Ltd**
Park Mill
Brougham Street
Skipton
North Yorks BD23 2JN
Tel: 01756 791313
Email: admin@proarte.co.uk
www.proarte.co.uk

## Raphael & Berge (brushes)

**Max Sauer SA**
2 Rue Lamarek, BP 204
22002 Saint-Brieuc
France
www.max-sauer.com

## Rexel Derwent
(watersoluble pencils)

**Acco-Rexel Ltd**
Gatehouse Road, Aylesbury
Bucks HP19 3DT
Tel: 01296 397444
www.acco.co.uk

## St Cuthbert's
(watercolour supports)

**St Cuthbert's Paper Mill**
Wells, Somerset BA5 IAG
Tel: 01749 672015
www.inveresk.co.uk

## Schminke
(watercolour and gouache paints)

**C. Roberson & Co**
1A Hercules Street
London N7 6AT
Tel: 0207 272 0567
www.robco.co.uk

## Sennelier
(watercolour paints & brushes)

**Tollit & Harvey Ltd**
Lyon Way
Greenford,
Middlesex UB6 OBN
www.sennelier.fr

## Talens (gouache paints & brushes)

**Royal Talens BV**
PO Box 4, 7300 AA Apeldoorn
The Netherlands
Tel: (55) 527 4700
www.talens.com

## Two Rivers (watercolour supports)

**Two Rivers Paper Co**
Pitt Mill, Roadwater
Watchet, Somerset TA23 OQS
Tel: 01984 641028

## Winsor & Newton
(gouache & watercolour paints, brushes)

**Winsor & Newton**
Whitefriars Avenue
Wealdstone
Harrow HA3 5RH
Tel: 0208 427 4343
www.winsornewton.com

# Index

Acknowledgements

# Acknowledgements

*The Collins Artist's Little Book of Watercolour* is based on material from *Collins Complete Artist's Manual*. © The copyright in the images reproduced in this book remains with the individual artists/successors, photographers, art material manufacturers and publishers, and is reproduced here by prior arrangement and/or kind permission. In case of any errors or omissions please contact the publishers for rectification in subsequent editions.

## Contributing artists:

Penny Anstice
Ray Balkwill
Ann Blockley
John Blockley
Hercules B. Brabazon
Jane Camp
Rosemary Carruthers
Trevor Chamberlain
William Dealtry
Geraldine Girvan
Gerald Green
Roy Hammond
Ken Howard
Albert Jackson
David Jackson
Simon Jennings
Ronald Jesty
Sally Keir
Sophie Knight
Edward McKnight
Kauffer
Alex McKibbin
John Lidzey
John Martin
John Mitchell
Fiona Peart
Patrick Procktor
Penny Quested
Jacqueline Rizvi
Hans Schwarz
Michael Stiff
David Suff
Robert Tilling
David Tindle
Shirley Trevena
J.M.W. Turner
Anna Wood
Leslie Worth